CONTENTS

PETERSEN AUTOMOTIVE BOOKS

LEE KELLEY/Editorial Director
KALTON C. LAHUE/Editor
SPENCE MURRAY/Automotive Editor
DAVID COHEN/Managing Editor
SUSIE VOLKMANN/Art Director
LINNEA HUNT-STEWART/Copy Editor
RAYMOND HARPER/Copy Editor
LINDA SARGENT/Copy Editor
FERN CASON/Editorial Coordinator

GENERAL MOTORS X-CARS TUNE-UP & REPAIR

ISBN 0-8227-5058-9
Library of Congress Catalog Card Number: 81-80246

PETERSEN PUBLISHING COMPANY

R.E. PETERSEN/Chairman of the Board; **F.R. WAINGROW**/President; **ROBERT E. BROWN**/Sr. Vice President, Publisher; **DICK DAY**/Sr. Vice President; **JIM P. WALSH**/Sr. Vice President, National Advertising Director; **ROBERT MacLEOD**/Vice President, Publisher; **THOMAS J. SIATOS**/Vice President, Group Publisher; **PHILIP E. TRIMBACH**/Vice President, Financial Administration; **WILLIAM PORTER**/Vice President, Circulation Director; **JAMES J. KRENEK**/Vice President, Manufacturing; **LEO D. LaREW**/Treasurer; **DICK WATSON**/Controller; **LOU ABBOTT**/Director, Production; **JOHN CARRINGTON**/Director, Book Sales and Marketing; **MARIA COX**/Director, Data Processing; **BOB D'OLIVO**/Director, Photography; **NIGEL P. HEATON**/Director, Circulation Marketing and Administration; **AL ISAACS**/Director, Corporate Art; **CAROL JOHNSON**/Director, Advertising Administration; **DON McGLATHERY**/Director, Advertising Research; **JACK THOMPSON**/Assistant Director, Circulation; **VERN BALL**/Director, Fulfillment Services

1
Introduction

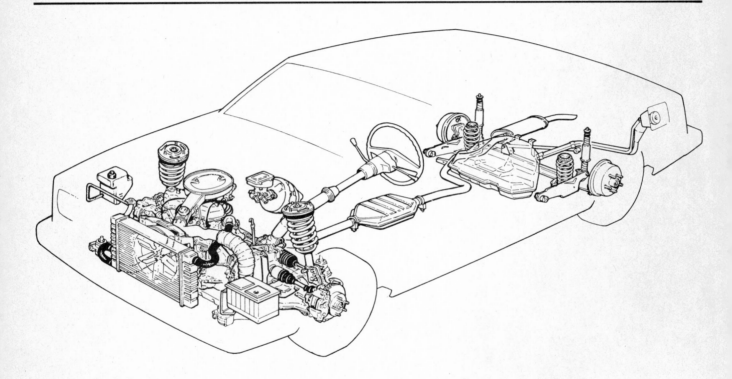

Congratulations! As the owner of a 1980-or-later Buick Skylark, Chevrolet Citation, Oldsmobile Omega, or Pontiac Phoenix (collectively referred to as X-cars), you are driving General Motors' answer to the recurring energy crises of recent years. Your X-car was designed to deliver superior gas mileage, but to keep it running at peak performance and to enjoy maximum fuel economy, it must be kept properly tuned and maintained.

Lift the hood of your X-car and compare what's in the engine compartment to your previous car. It will probably appear quite uncomplicated by comparison, but looks can be deceiving—don't think you can neglect under-hood service. Both 4 and 6-cylinder engines are equipped with the latest emissions control systems, and while they may look simple, these systems can't do their job unless your engine is correctly tuned and maintained. To do this properly, you must know what these systems are, where they are located, and how they work. To help you with this particular problem, we've included a chapter on the X-car emissions systems.

General Motors' dealers will service your X-car according to a factory-prescribed maintenance schedule, which differs considerably from the tune-up procedure such shops once followed. Our procedure (see the Tune-up chapter) is essentially a *basic* tune-up, and includes steps and tests that should be performed each time the engine is tuned. Remember, an engine tune-up is *preventive* maintenance—if done properly and at regular intervals, you should enjoy thousands of trouble-free miles from your X-car. It's up to you to establish how often the procedure is performed, but we strongly recommend it every 7500 miles.

Following our basic tune-up procedure will assure good engine performance—a primary consideration in good fuel economy. You can probably in-

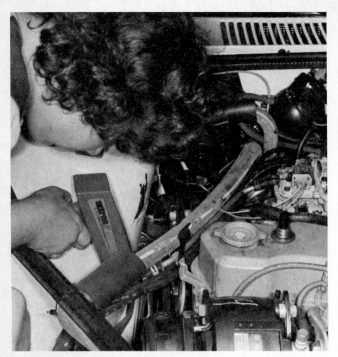

You can't do without a timing light. While connecting the test leads is easy, locating the timing marks on the pulley under the maze of belts and hoses is more difficult.

crease your mpg even further by taking a good look at your personal driving habits. We all have a few bad ones, and by substituting good driving habits in their place, you can often squeeze more miles from a gallon of gasoline.

Tests and Equipment

Keeping any automobile in good running condition involves a certain amount of testing—either as part of the regular tune-up procedure or when troubleshooting system malfunctions. In fact, you'll find references to certain test procedures sprinkled throughout the following chapters. Old hands at do-it-yourself car care will recognize the tests, having performed them countless times before. Those who are new to maintaining their car, however, may not (1) know what the test is, (2) understand how to perform it, or (3) be able to interpret the results properly. To help those readers, the common test procedures necessary to properly maintain an X-car are presented below in alphabetical order.

You'll need certain tune-up and test equipment to perform these tests. You should have a *timing light,* a *compression tester,* a *vacuum/pressure gauge,* and a *multifunction ignition analyzer.* A *remote start switch* is also handy; when properly connected to the starter solenoid, it allows you to crank and/or start the engine from under the hood—a time-saving convenience. Now, let's look at the various tests.

Compression Test

Since this test measures the amount of pressure in a cylinder during the compression stroke while the engine is cranking, it can tell you a good deal about your engine. If the compression in one or more cylinders is low or uneven, the engine cannot be tuned satisfactorily until the problem is corrected. The cause of low compression may be valve malfunctioning, worn or broken piston rings, or even a damaged piston.

Before running a compression test, make sure that the battery is in good shape and fully charged. Remove the spark plugs, connect your remote start switch, and disconnect the ignition harness at the distributor. This will prevent the engine from starting and protect the electronic module from any possible damage while allowing you to "crank" the engine. Install the compression tester in the No. 1 spark plug hole, and hold the throttle wide open while you crank the engine over for at least five compression strokes. Record the gauge reading and release the pressure relief valve on the compression tester: then, repeat the procedure for each remaining cylinder.

Compare the compression readings to factory specifications. Compression readings for an engine in good condition should not vary more than 15 psi from the highest to the lowest reading, although General Motors recommends that the lowest cylinder be at least 80 percent of the highest reading. If you have a lower reading cylinder, it's a good idea to run a cranking vacuum test to determine the cause.

Cranking Vacuum Test

This test uses the vacuum gauge and will determine the cause of low cylinder compression. To prepare the engine for the test, back off any throttle stops to close the throttle completely. Plug the vacuum line running from the carburetor to the PCV valve and any other lines which allow air to enter the intake manifold.

Connect your vacuum gauge to the intake manifold—"T-ing" it into the vacuum brake booster line will do the trick. Make sure the HEI distributor is disabled as in the compression test above; then, use

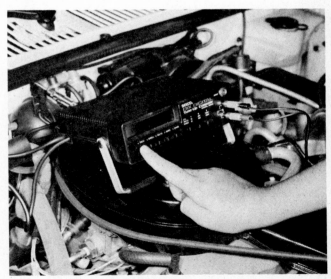

Small home-type tune-up equipment such as this Dix Digital Tune-Up Computer will handle most of the tune-up problems you'll encounter.

Introduction

the remote starter switch to crank the engine for about 10 seconds while you watch the vacuum gauge needle. A good-sealing engine will develop a reading of about 5 inches Hg. A lower reading obtained at a normal cranking speed indicates worn piston rings.

The vacuum gauge will tell you other things about your engine's internal condition. Reconnect the HEI distributor to the ignition harness and hook up an engine tachometer. Start the engine and let it idle. Note the reading and then slowly increase engine speed, watching the action of the gauge needle. Here's how to interpret the readings:

(a) A slowly fluctuating reading indicates an idle mixture that's too lean.

(b) A low but steady reading indicates retarded valve or ignition timing.

(c) An intermittent drop in vacuum indicates a sticking or leaking valve.

(d) A steady reading at idle which fluctuates rapidly at higher rpm indicates weak valve springs.

(e) Continuous rapid fluctuation of the needle at all speeds indicates a defective head gasket.

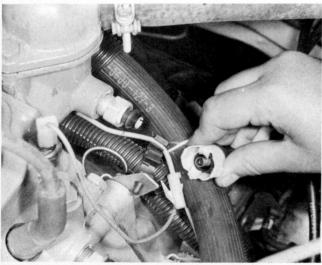

X-cars equipped with the C-4 emissions system have a lot of strange-looking devices. You might mistake this one for the temperature indicator switch, since it's installed in the thermostat housing, but it's the sensor for the electronic module.

Cranking Voltage Test

Testing the battery, charging, and starting systems at regular intervals can help locate potential trouble before it develops. A battery test, for example, will definitely pinpoint a weak or failing battery, while a check of the charging system voltage and current output will give you a clue that something is wrong. If the alternator won't deliver full output, further checks and tests should be made, instead of waiting until there's absolutely no charge.

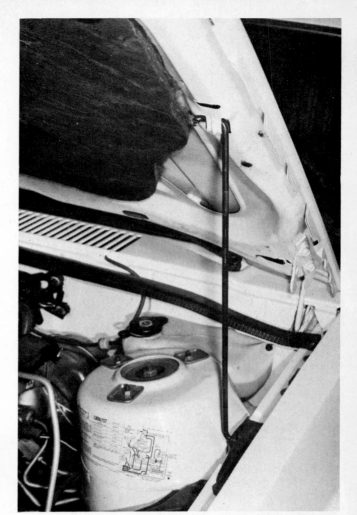

Some models are equipped with this side-mounted hood arm; others have it located at the front of the engine compartment.

The cranking voltage test will check both battery condition and starter operation. Connect the positive (red) lead of your ignition analyzer to the positive (+) battery terminal and the negative (black) lead to the negative (-) battery terminal. Set the analyzer on the voltmeter function. Crank the engine with the remote start switch while reading the scale and listening to the starter's cranking speed. Do not crank the engine for more than 15 seconds at a time.

The scale should read at least 9.6 volts and the starter should crank the engine uniformly at a good rate of speed. A borderline or low reading, or a starter that sounds sluggish, indicates a weak battery or excessive starter current draw.

Current Output Test

This test will tell you if the alternator is sending sufficient current to the battery to keep it fully charged. Your ignition analyzer should have a battery post adapter which is required for this test. Remove the linkage switch from the adapter, and install the shunt lever/lead with the lever in its closed position.

Set the analyzer to read amps, and disable the HEI distributor by disconnecting the ignition har-

The 4-cylinder engine air cleaner is attached with two nuts. Tighten them equally but don't overtighten or you may warp the carburetor air horn.

ness at the distributor cap. Switch the car's headlamps on for about three minutes; then, crank the engine for 15 seconds to reduce battery voltage. Turn off the headlamps, and reconnect the ignition harness to the HEI distributor.

Start the engine, and set the fast idle cam on its second step while reading the amperage scale on the analyzer. Add 5-10 amps to the reading to compensate for ignition system draw and compare the reading to the alternator's rated output (X-car alternators are rated at 42, 63, or 70 amps, depending upon equipment). If your amperage reading falls within ±3 amps of the rated output, the alternator is delivering maximum output to the battery.

Distributor Advance Checks

Distributor advance can be checked in one of two ways: by a functional test or by the timing light (dynamic) test. The functional test tells you only if the advance mechanisms are in proper working order—it will not tell you whether the amount of advance present at a given rpm is within factory specifications.

To perform the functional test, remove the HEI distributor cap. Open the centrifugal advance weights as far as possible with your fingers, and then release them. The weights should snap smoothly back into position. If they do not, the mechanism is either dirty or the springs have lost some of their tension.

Now disconnect the vacuum line at the vacuum advance diaphragm. Connect a hand vacuum pump or a small length of vacuum hose to the diaphragm fitting and draw a vacuum. If you use a vacuum pump, draw about 10 inches Hg. Without a pump, suck as hard on the line with your mouth as you can and pinch it off with a pair of pliers. This will hold the vacuum in the line. If the advance mechanism is working properly, the linkage from the diaphragm

will move the magnetic pickup when the vacuum is applied.

The dynamic test is more useful since it tells you how well the mechanism is working at engine speeds above idle. Hook an engine tachometer to the distributor pigtail marked "TACH" and a good engine ground. Connect your timing light leads to the battery terminals (red to +, black to -) and to the No. 1 spark plug. Start the engine and point the light at the timing mark on the front pulley. Note the reading and compare it to the specifications—this is the initial timing setting.

An ignition firing indicator is used to locate a bad plug wire. You'll see a bright flash in the indicator window when the plug fires if the wire is okay. A weak flash, or no flash, indicates that the wire is defective.

Disconnect the vacuum line from the distributor vacuum advance unit and plug the line. Gradually increase engine speed to 2000 rpm, then to 4000 rpm. Note the setting at each speed, subtract the initial advance, and what remains is centrifugal advance.

Return the engine to idle, and reconnect the vacuum line to the vacuum advance diaphragm fitting. Note the reading at idle, and then gradually in-

Expensive or complicated tune-up equipment is not necessary. This Suntune inductive dwell-tach works fine with either X-car engine.

Introduction

crease engine speed again, just as you did to read centrifugal advance. Subtract the combined initial and centrifugal advance from the total advance at each speed and what remains is vacuum advance. Comparing these figures to the specifications provided in the Tune-up chapter will tell you how accurately both advance mechanisms are working.

Proper starter operation is important. If replacement is necessary, it's done from under the car.

Ignition Timing Check

Instructions and specifications for checking and adjusting the engine's initial timing will be found on the tune-up or emissions decal in the engine compartment. The procedure is quite simple, as it involves connecting the timing light leads to the battery and the No. 1 spark plug, as in the distributor advance check sequence.

Start the engine and aim the light at the timing mark pointer above the pulley. A notched line on the harmonic balancer or pulley should align with the pointer mark. If it does not, the timing must be adjusted. Loosen the distributor hold-down clamp bolt at the base of the distributor. Keep your eye on the pointer/mark and slowly rotate the distributor until the two align properly. Tighten the hold-down bolt and recheck the timing mark alignment with the timing light.

The procedure is easy enough, but reaching the distributor on the L4 engine to rotate it can be a two-man job due to its location at the rear side of the engine near the intake manifold. The V6 distributor is positioned right on top of the intake manifold near the carburetor, and can be adjusted by one person.

Radiator Pressure Test

To check the cooling system for leakage, remove the pressure cap from the filler neck and run the engine until it is at normal operating temperature. Shut the engine off and connect a pressure tester in place of the radiator cap. The pressure tester is a hand-operated pump fitted with a pressure gauge. By operating the tester handle, you can apply pressure to the cooling system.

Apply 15 psi pressure and watch the gauge needle. If the cooling system is O.K. and has no leaks, the needle will remain steady for at least 2 minutes. Should the needle begin to drop slowly, look for a small leak(s) in the form of a loose clamp, poor connection, or leaking gasket. Any hose that swells under pressure is weak and should be replaced.

If the gauge needle drops quickly after pressure is applied, or if it fluctuates considerably, there's a combustion leak. This usually takes the form of a defective head gasket. To locate the cylinder where the leak occurs, short out each spark plug one at a time by removing its cable briefly. When the leaking plug's cable is removed, the needle will stop fluctuating.

The cooling system may test out satisfactorily, but

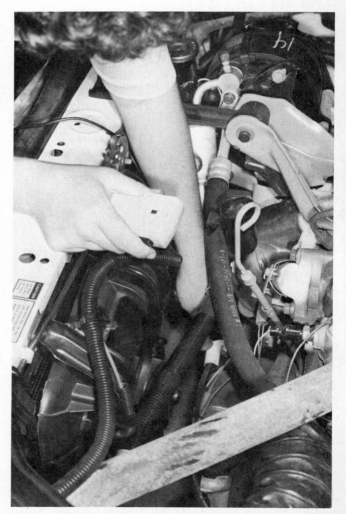

It's not exactly easy, but you can connect a remote starter button to the starter solenoid. This allows you to crank the engine from the engine compartment.

A hand vacuum pump can be used to test the air cleaner door operation.

VIN and How to Find It

The Vehicle Identification Number (VIN) is the legal identification of your X-car. It is found on a plate attached to the left top of the instrument panel and can be easily read through the windshield from outside the car. The VIN is also found on your title and registration certificates. The fifth character of the VIN is the engine code. This code may be necessary when ordering certain replacement parts.

Establish a Procedure

Some or all of these tests and checks should be performed during a normal tune-up. If you find a reference to a test or check in our pictorial tune-up sequences later in the book, refer back to this chapter for the detailed explanation necessary for carrying out the test/check.

Additionally, our basic tune-up recommendations for improved gas mileage and a better-running engine follow a definite sequence, and so should yours. While you may prefer to rearrange the steps involved, you should follow a logical sequence to avoid jumping from one end of the engine compartment to the other. Such organization will reduce both the time and effort required.

Along with a minimum number of tools, test equipment, and the specifications needed for tuning your engine, you should keep on hand a spare set of plugs, a fan belt, and other spare parts so you'll know where to find them when needed. Whether you're a first-timer or an old hand at tuning an engine, this book will increase your knowledge and make you more proficient at keeping your X-car in top operating condition. And after all, that's the bottom line—an engine that operates at its peak efficiency and economy.

don't forget that the cap itself can be defective. Coolant system pressure testers are equipped with a cap adapter. This is attached to the tester and the radiator cap fitted in place on the adapter. The cap should hold its rated pressure for 30 seconds or longer if it's in good condition. A gauge needle that falls rapidly indicates a defective cap, which should be replaced with a new one of the same type and rating.

The engine support strut keeps the engine from torquing over under load. Worn bushings in the strut will require replacement.

Proper plug wire routing is important to prevent damage to the insulation from heat or abrasion.

2

Lube and Maintenance

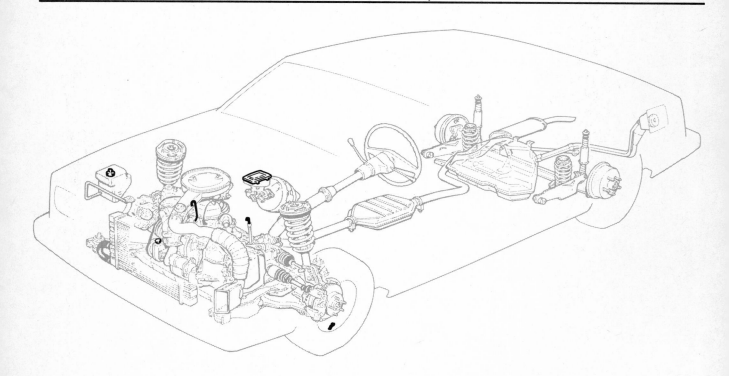

Domestic car manufacturers (including GM) have not specified a daily maintenance procedure for many years, nor is one absolutely necessary. But a brief daily inspection *is* in order if you wish to catch small problems before they become large ones. The best time to give the car a quick once-over is in the morning, after the car has been sitting all night.

Walk slowly around the car and check the tires before you get in. If one appears noticeably lower than the rest, check it with a pressure gauge. When the tire is only a few pounds under its proper pressure, it can be reinflated at a nearby service station on your way to work. Recheck the pressure before you start home. If the loss is repeated, you have a slow leak either in the tire itself or in the valve. Don't take chances—have the tire serviced.

Next on your inspection, look under the car for any signs of liquid. If you park your car in a garage

at night, back it out of the garage and check the garage floor. Your daily inspection is finished if there are no telltale signs of leaks. But suppose you find a puddle that wasn't there yesterday. The first thing to do is identify the liquid. It can only be one of seven different types, and the accompanying chart shows you what to do for each.

Seals that leak slightly can be left in place until you can have them replaced—except those on the brake system, which demand immediate repair. Just be aware of them and check the appropriate fluid reservoir or sump more frequently than normal. Make a check of the level of a known leaking fluid a part of your daily inspection. For example, if you know that the water pump is throwing a little coolant from the pump shaft seal, lift the hood during your daily walk-around. Check the radiator's coolant expansion tank and add a little fluid to replace what has been lost. Any increase in the amount of fluid

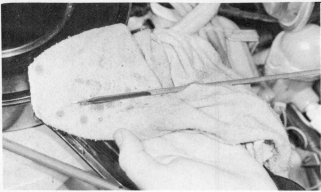

Allow your car to sit at least three minutes with the engine off before you check the oil level with the dipstick. If the car isn't level, your reading will not be accurate.

required indicates that the seal is finally failing completely and should be replaced immediately.

Looking under your X-car a few minutes after driving it hard on a hot day, you may find puddles caused by two unusual conditions. The first involves the air conditioning system. Even in a dry climate, the cooling coils will condense water vapor from the air, but this vapor is normally blown away as long as the car is moving. But when the car is stopped, the coils continue to condense water vapor for a short period. This condensation will form a puddle of water under the vehicle.

The second unusual circumstance concerns a leak in the coolant recovery line. Stopping a hot engine can cause localized boiling of the coolant in the engine block. This raises the cooling system pressure high enough to force open the spring-loaded relief valve in the radiator cap. When this happens, a quantity of coolant will gush out the overflow tube before the pressure drops sufficiently for the relief valve to pop back in place. If you find a puddle of coolant on the garage floor, check the coolant recovery line. It may be damaged or deteriorated to the point of leaking. If this is the case, replacing the line will solve the problem.

Weekly Inspections

A more thorough inspection should be performed every week. The routine will not take much longer than your daily inspection. This is the time to check the fluid reservoirs and take a look at other points in the car's mechanisms.

Make sure that the car is level, and open the hood. Check the brake system first, as it is the most critical. Like all current American cars, X-cars use a dual brake system. One front wheel and the rear wheel on the opposite side form one system; the other front wheel and its opposite at the rear form the other. There is no connection between the two except through the brake pedal, which operates both systems at the same time. The master cylinder is a dual-function unit which contains a reservoir for each of the systems.

The brake master cylinder, which contains the hydraulic fluid reservoirs, is located on the driver's side in the engine compartment and just above the steering column. It may or may not have a drum-

shaped canister between it and the firewall. If it does, this means that your X-car has power-assisted brakes as one of its options. The power-assist unit has no bearing on checking the fluid level.

Unsnap the top, look inside, and make sure that the fluid levels are at the point specified in your owner's manual or marked on the outside of the reservoir itself. If not, add enough brake fluid to bring the level up to the full mark or to the top of the reservoir divider. General Motors recommends you use only Delco Supreme No. 11 brake fluid or its equivalent, but you can use any good fluid which conforms to SAE Specification 70R3.

Brake fluid is "hygroscopic," meaning it will absorb water from the water vapor in the air if exposed to the atmosphere over a period of time. Since water will ruin the performance of brake fluid, you should never use any which has been kept in an open container or a container which has been opened and closed frequently.

The master cylinder reservoir level will gradually drop as brake wear takes place. You may not realize that the level has dropped slightly if you check the brake fluid after the car has been driven. Brake fluid absorbs heat from the brakes and expands, so make it a point to check the fluid level before driving the car, not after.

The cooling system is next. All X-cars are factory-equipped with a coolant recovery system, and the fluid level should be checked on the plastic expansion tank—do not remove the radiator cap to check coolant level. Keep a close eye on the area around the radiator cap, however. If the cap fails, it will allow coolant to escape.

The engine oil and automatic transaxle fluid have their own dipsticks. Engine oil should be checked with the engine off and cold, but the automatic transaxle fluid should be checked with the engine on and running at idle and normal operating temperature. To check the fluid level of a manual transaxle, you'll either have to crawl under the car or raise the car on a hoist. Don't jack the front end up,

Proper accessory fluid levels are important. Keep an eye on those hard-to-get-at units, such as the L4 power steering pump, and top up when required.

as the transaxle will no longer be level and your reading will be incorrect.

The manual transaxle filler hole plug is used both to check the fluid level and to add fluid. This plug is located on the left side of the driveaxle case above the axle shaft. If the transaxle is hot, lubricant may flow from the hole when you remove the plug. For this reason, you should check the fluid level when the transaxle is cold. The fluid should be barely level with the filler plug hole when cool. If it is not, add Dexron II automatic transmission fluid to bring the fluid level with the hole, and then replace the plug snugly. Unless you have a leak, it is not necessary to check the manual transaxle fluid level more frequently than every six months.

The power steering pump also has its own hydraulic fluid reservoir. On the 4-cylinder engine, the pump is located underneath the air conditioning compressor at the front of the engine on the passenger's side. You'll need a small arm to reach between the maze of hoses and wiring, remove the cap, and then bring it up and out of the engine compartment to check the dipstick level. The V6 power steering pump is located on the same side as the L4, but at the back of the engine, and is not as difficult to reach.

If the power steering pump fluid is hot, it should register between the "hot" and "cold" marks on the dipstick. When the fluid is cool, it should be between the "cold" and "add" marks. If the fluid level is low, add sufficient power steering fluid to bring it to the proper level. General Motors recommends GM Power Steering Fluid GM-1050017 or an equivalent product.

Don't overlook the windshield washer reservoir. In cold weather, use an alcohol/water mixture to prevent freezing. During warm weather, plain water with a little liquid detergent added is satisfactory, although you can buy "special" washer fluids.

Once you've finished with the fluid reservoirs, check the drivebelts. They should be tight, but not too tight. You need the proper amount of slack between pulleys. To determine if you have it, grasp a belt midway between the pulleys. You should be able to press it down about ⅜ inch. If the car has been running hot but the coolant level is correct, the alternator belt is probably too loose. Any unnecessary slack in this belt will cause overheating, since it drives the water pump. It will also cause undercharging, which can gradually destroy your battery. Check the underside of each belt for cracks and splits or other defects. If you find any, make it a point to replace the belt as soon as possible.

Hoses leak through cracks and loose joints. The latter are slow leaks, while cracks often cause catastrophic ruptures. Check the hoses carefully and frequently, as they harden with age and may crack if moved from their normal position. Exceptions to this rule are the upper and lower radiator hoses, which betray advancing age by turning soft and mushy. As soon as your hoses show these warning signs, replace them immediately to prevent a failure

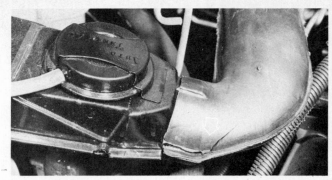

Engine vibration has a tendency to crack the plastic air duct (arrow). Such leaks upset the operation of the Thermac air cleaner and adversely affect engine operation.

on the road. (Further information on cooling system care is provided in the chapter starting on page 88.)

While you're working under the hood, check the condition and routing of vacuum lines. These small hoses are subjected to the same amount of heat as radiator hoses, and will often turn brittle and crack with age. If you find any suspicious looking lines, replace them now and save yourself the problem of troubleshooting the malfunction they're bound to cause later.

Any leaks in the exhaust system can be detected by a noticeable increase in exhaust noise. Although the car will run satisfactorily in this condition, leaks should be corrected as soon as possible, since deadly carbon monoxide fumes can seep into the car's interior.

Check the condition and operation of all lights. Inspect the lenses for cracks or other damage, and pay particular attention to brake lights and turn signals. While it helps to have someone else tell you if everything works when you operate the controls, you can do this yourself simply by backing up close to a light-colored wall, especially at night, and looking through the rear-view mirror to see any difference in the brightness of taillights, brakelights, turn signals, and back-up lights.

The real value of regular inspections such as those outlined above is the regularity—you know the daily needs of your car. By discovering and correcting small problems while they're still small, you can save a great deal of time, money, and effort.

Know the location of the fuse box and keep spare fuses in the car. The first troubleshooting procedure for any electrical problem is to check the fuse.

Driveway Puddles

Liquid	Characteristics	Sources	Check	Action
Gasoline	Thin, nonviscous, highly volatile, strong odor	Carburetor	Fuel line connections	Tighten
			Stuck/damaged float or needle valve	Tap carb with plastic hammer while engine is running. If leak persists, stop engine, remove carb top cover and investigate.
		Fuel filter	Connections	Tighten
			Gasket (if any)	Tighten screws; if leak persists, replace gasket.
		Fuel lines	Connections	Tighten
			Splits, cracks	Replace line
		Fuel pump	Connections	Tighten
			Gasket	Tighten screws; if leak persists, replace gasket.
		Fuel tank	Connections	Tighten
			Tank seams or pinhole in tank body	Run bar of soap along seam or hole to temporarily stop leak. Tank must be removed and replaced/repaired.
Brake fluid	Honey-colored, oily, attacks paint	Reservoir	Connections	Tighten
		Master cylinder	Connections	Tighten
		Wheel cylinders	Seals	Replace
			Connections	Tighten
		Brake lines	Seals	Replace
			Connections	Tighten
Automatic transaxle fluid	Honey-colored, oily, less viscous than oil	Automatic transaxle	Pan gasket	Tighten pan nuts; if leak persists, replace gasket.
			Seals	Replace
			Transaxle cooler	Tighten connections
Hydraulic fluid	Similar to brake fluid.	Power steering unit	Reservoir	Add as required; tighten connections.
			Pump	Tighten connections; replace any leaking seal.
			Lines	Tighten connections
			Seals	Replace
			Connections	Tighten
Water	Transparent, not slippery, no odor	Cooling system (if water used as coolant)	Radiator	Fill; if leaking, have repaired.
			Expansion tank	Same as above.
			Hoses	Replace
			Hose connections	Tighten
			Freeze plugs	Replace
			Water pump gasket	Tighten bolts; if leak persists, replace gasket.
			Water pump seal	Replace
		Windshield washer system	Bottle, lines	Fill; if leaking, replace.
		Air conditioner	Bottom of cooling coil	If water drips inside car, install drain line; if it drips outside car, ignore.
		Heater	Hoses	Replace
			Hose connections	Tighten
Coolant (water/ glycol mixture)	Brightly colored (usually green), watery but slippery, slight odor	Cooling system	Same as water.	Same as water.
Oil	Dark, viscous, oil, slight odor	Engine	Sump dipstick	Add as required.
			Oil pan gasket	Tighten pan bolts.
			Front and rear crankshaft seals	Replace if leaking profusely.

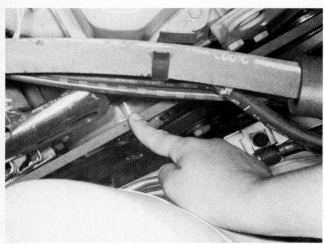

1. Start your maintenance check at the right-hand rear of the engine compartment. Depress the fan belt and check the amount of deflection. It should deflect about ⅜ inch.

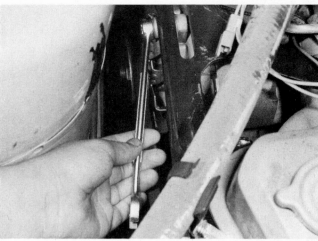

2. If the belt tension requires adjustment, loosen the mounting bracket bolt shown here and move the alternator in the appropriate direction; then retighten the bolt.

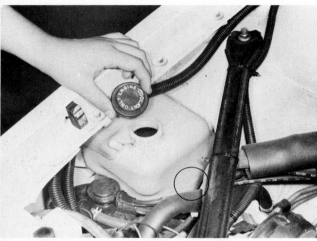

3. Check the coolant level and condition at the recovery bottle—not the radiator. Coolant should be clean and clear in appearance, and not exceed the line on the bottle (circled).

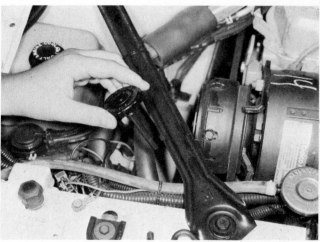

4. Reach under the air conditioning compressor and locate the power steering pump. Remove the cap and withdraw it from the pump. Check the dipstick level, and replace the cap.

5. Remove the radiator cap and inspect the cap ears and gaskets, and check the filler neck seats for distortion.

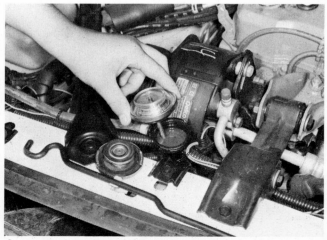

6. If you have radiator/thermostat problems, a coolant thermometer will help you diagnose the cause. Run the engine for 15-20 minutes and read the thermometer dial.

7. Retighten the rocker arm cover bolts to prevent oil leaks and wipe the cover clean. If you have a torque wrench, the correct torque value is 6 ft.-lbs.

8. Remove the air cleaner and check the carburetor mounting nuts. You can tighten them snugly with an open-end wrench; the correct torque value is 60 in.-lbs.

9. Operate the choke linkage and spray with WD-40 or a similar solvent to free any sticking parts. This treatment will lubricate the linkage and prevent future sticking.

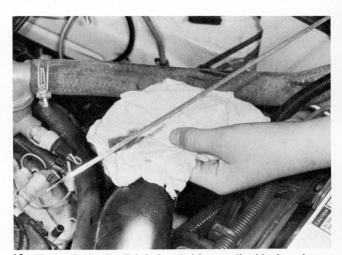

10. The engine's dipstick is located low on the block under the thermostat housing. Pull it out and wipe clean; then reinsert. Pull it out again and check the oil level/condition.

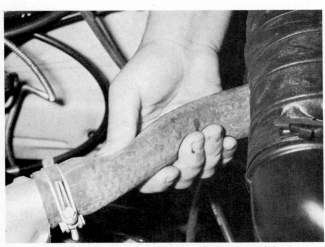

11. Flex the upper radiator hose by squeezing it gently and check for deterioration. If the hose feels mushy, it should be replaced without delay to prevent a failure on the road.

12. Check each hose connection and tighten the clamp if necessary. This will prevent future leaks. The lower radiator hose must be checked and tightened from under the car.

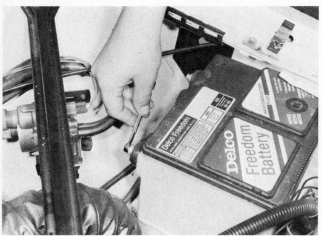

13. *Check the battery clamp condition and tighten if necessary. Poor contact or corrosion here will cause a "no-start" condition. A 7mm wrench will do the job.*

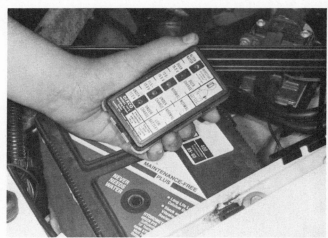

14. *Test the battery with a charging system tester like this Dixco unit. Its light-emitting diode (LED) system will tell you the condition of your battery and alternator.*

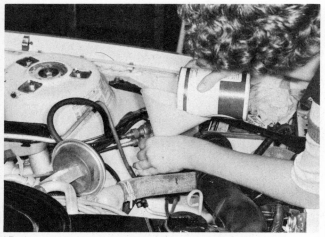

15. *If your X-car is equipped with an automatic transaxle, remove and check the dipstick. To add fluid, you'll need a funnel with a long and/or flexible neck. Add fluid in small quantities and recheck.*

16. *Pop off the master cylinder cover and check the fluid level in each reservoir compartment. Add fresh fluid if necessary to bring level up to divider.*

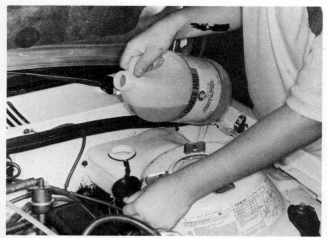

17. *Check the windshield washer reservoir level. Keep it topped up with a mixture of clear water and windshield cleaner. In cold weather, use an additive to prevent freezing.*

18. *Wipe the hood latch assembly clean and relubricate with a dry lube stick such as Door-Ease; then lubricate the hood hinges with a few drops of engine oil.*

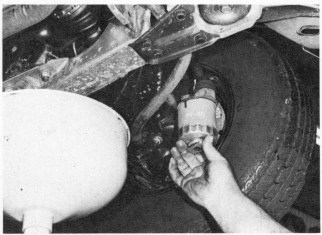

19. The screw-on throwaway oil filter is located beside the fuel pump at the bottom rear of the engine. The cap-type filter tool shown here does the removal job best.

20. Lubricate the rubber seal on the new oil filter with a thin coat of engine oil before installing it. Do not overtighten the filter or removing it next time will be difficult.

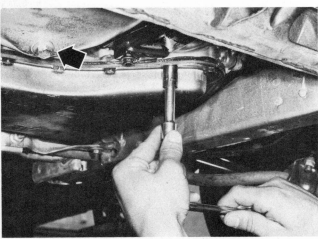

21. Check the transaxle pan bolts and retighten if necessary to prevent fluid leaks. Wipe the pan clean. To change the engine oil, remove the drain plug (arrow).

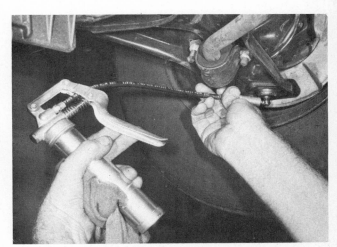

22. There are two suspension/steering linkage lubrication fittings at each wheel. Use a water-resistant EP chassis lubricant every 7500 miles.

23. A few sprays of WD-40 on the rubber suspension bushings will keep them flexible and reduce their tendency to squeak. Be sure to do the same at the rear suspension.

24. Use a reliable tire pressure gauge and check air pressure with the tire cold. Capacity depends upon type of tire, and will be found on tire casing.

1. The V6 air cleaner is simple to remove compared to the L4 version. Remove the cover and filter, disconnect the fresh air tube, and remove the Pulsair tubes from the valves.

2. Check the carburetor for the air horn-to-air cleaner gasket. If it is missing or damaged, install a new one. This gasket prevents air leaks and is important in achieving the correct air/fuel ratio.

3. Check the carburetor mounting nuts for tightness. Engine vibration can loosen these nuts sufficiently to cause a vacuum leak and adversely affect driveability.

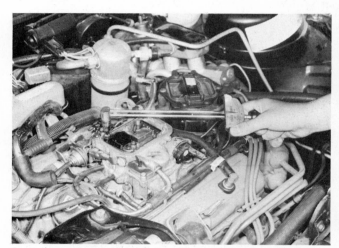

4. Also check the air horn attaching screws. If loose, tighten the screws securely in an alternating pattern. Using a torque wrench will prevent overtightening the screws.

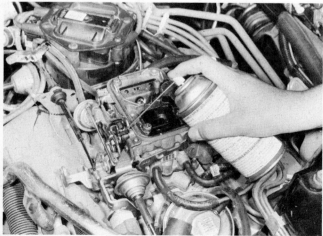

5. Work the choke butterfly back and forth by hand; then apply a few sprays of WD-40 to clean and lubricate the linkage for continued proper operation.

6. Step to the passenger's side of the engine compartment and locate the drive belt. Depress the belt in the center between the pulleys to check the tension. The belt should deflect 3/8 inch.

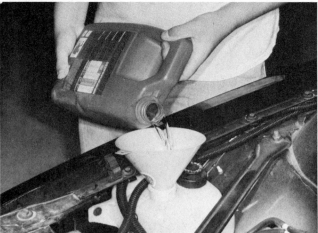

7. Visually inspect the coolant level in the recovery bottle. If it is below the specified level, add sufficient coolant/water mixture to restore the fluid to the correct level.

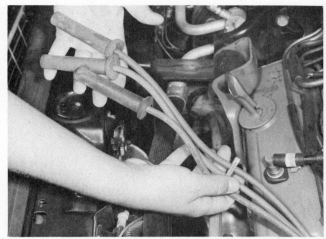

8. Inspect the spark plug cables for signs of deterioration, abrasion, or other damage. Make sure cables are routed to avoid touching accessory units.

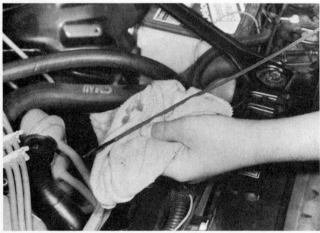

9. Reach down by the Pulsair valve and remove the crankcase dipstick. Wipe clean, reinsert, and withdraw it to check the oil level. The engine must be cold for proper reading.

10. If the oil level is below the hatched mark on the dipstick, here's where the oil is added. GM recommends only SE-quality oil and suggests a 7500-mile interval for changes.

11. Check the radiator cap for gasket condition. If the gaskets are dried out, the cap should be replaced with one of the same type. The cap is rated at a system pressure of 15 psi.

12. It's a good idea to keep an eye on coolant condition as well as level, especially in cold weather areas. A coolant tester will tell you if the antifreeze/water mixture is correct.

13. When replacing the radiator cap, it must be installed with the arrows pointing horizontally. Follow instructions on the cap to avoid a painful burn.

14. While you're right in front of the engine, check the heater and radiator hose clamps. These are common leak points and may require periodic tightening of the clamp screws.

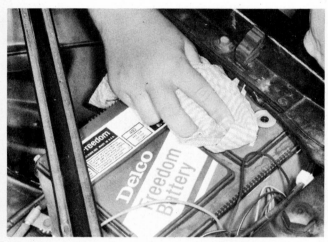

15. Wipe the battery case clean of any conductive charge material that may build up. The built-in hydrometer will tell you the overall battery condition.

16. If corrosion has built up on cable clamps, remove and clean them. A 7mm wrench will do the job. Do not overtighten the clamp screws, as this will internally damage the battery.

17. Keep an eye open for problems like this. The battery was replaced with the horn wire caught under it. Battery corrosion can thus affect horn operation.

18. Connect a voltmeter and crank the engine to check the battery. It should put out at least 9.6 volts during cranking; if not, you need a new battery.

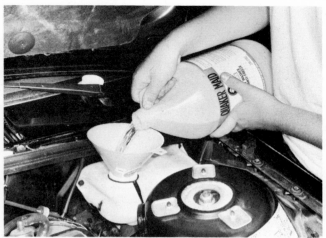

19. Check the windshield washer reservoir and fill to within an inch of the top with a mixture of water and washer fluid. In cold weather, use washer fluid full-strength.

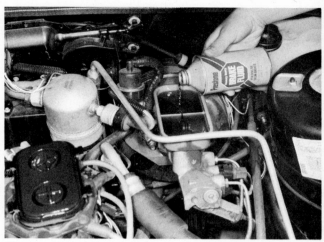

20. Pop off the master cylinder cover and check the brake fluid level. If necessary, top up with DOT 3 fluid from a fresh can, and replace the top on the master cylinder.

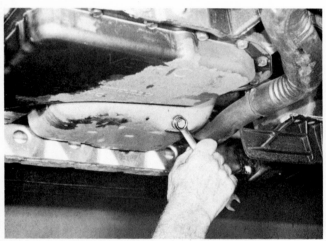

21. To change engine oil, remove the oil pan drain plug. If equipped with an automatic transaxle, tighten the transaxle pan bolts at the same time.

22. The oil filter is located at the front of the engine, just left of the starter. Use a cap-type filter tool as shown and turn counterclockwise to remove.

23. Smear a thin coat of oil on new filter gasket and install by hand. Do not overtighten or the filter will be very hard to remove next time around.

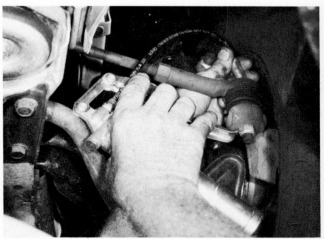

24. X-cars all have the same lubrication fitting points, regardless of the engine type. A small hand grease gun and flexible connector hose works out best in tight spots like this.

3
Tune-up Procedures

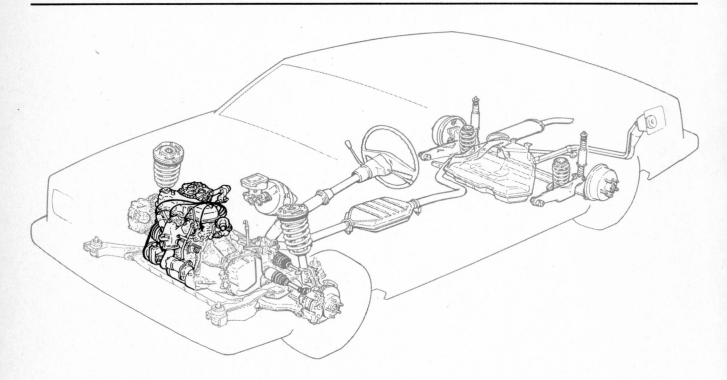

The key to keeping any car in good running order is a regular tune-up done properly. And while your X-car's 4 or 6-cylinder (V6) powerplant has earned a well-deserved reputation for being a hardy beast of burden, a tune-up is still necessary preventive maintenance. As such, it should be performed *before* the engine begins to cough and sputter. Additionally, the good mileage you expect from your X-car can be delivered only when everything has been properly cared for.

You may decide either to do your own tune-up and maintenance work or let someone else do it for you. If you don't do it yourself, we strongly advise you skip the corner garage and take it to an authorized GM dealership. There are two excellent reasons for this. First, a mechanic who has gone to school to learn the ins and outs of GM products and who works on cars exactly like yours every day is better able to deal with those perplexing little prob-

lems that are part of troubleshooting various components. In a word, the more *knowledgeable* mechanic is more efficient, is less likely to do work that has to be redone, and will turn the job out at a lower overall cost to the customer. Second, you're far less likely to run into problems when factory replacement parts are installed. Sure, you may save a few dollars here and there by buying independent parts when they're available, but they may not be equivalent in quality to genuine GM parts.

For Do-It-Yourselfers

If you have worked on other cars, you'll have no great difficulty working on your X-car, but you will have to learn how to work in much closer quarters. The transverse engine packaging in the engine compartment limits access to some important components and will require both extra time and patience to perform maintenance operations properly.

Be sure to follow the instructions on the emissions decal. This is located inside the engine compartment, along with a vacuum hose routing diagram. Each model year is subject to revisions or running changes in specifications and procedures. While we can provide you with the specifications which the factory used at the beginning of the model year, there's no guarantee that your particular model won't have some modifications that require different settings or adjustment procedures. If you refer to the decal and follow its specified procedures and adjustment settings, there will be no opportunity to go wrong.

To work on your X-car properly, you'll need a certain amount of tune-up and test equipment. While you can tune any engine with little more than a rusty wrench and a bent screwdriver, your adjustments are bound to be hit-or-miss, and you won't be able to diagnose conditions that are just developing which could cause a breakdown later on. If you've been shopping for tune-up and test equipment lately, you've probably noticed that the market is flooded with all kinds of goodies recommended as being invaluable for the do-it-yourselfer. But if you know what you need and what to look for, you can assemble a basic kit without spending a fortune. Start with a vacuum gauge, compression tester, timing light, tachometer, and voltmeter. These will get you by most test circumstances, but you'll probably want an engine analyzer or multimeter later.

Working on your own car requires the proper tools—and this means an investment. You may already have a toolbox full, but remember that the X-cars use *metric* fasteners, so you'll need metric tools. In addition to the basic and necessary wrenches, screwdrivers, and sockets, there are many other inexpensive specialty tools that can be a real help at times.

For example, there are many types of oil filter wrenches on the market, but in areas of limited clearance, the cap-type wrench which can be rotated with a socket works the best. Pick up a pair of insulated spark plug cable pullers. These let you get a solid grip on the protective boot without pulling on the wire and damaging the resistance core inside. They'll also prevent getting burned by a hot valve cover, and with the limited clearance around the V6 engine, they'll save the skin on your knuckles. If you plan on doing any internal work—engine or transaxle rebuild, clutch overhaul, oil seal replacement—you'll need a good torque wrench. (Torque, in this case, is the force required on a fastener to produce the necessary amount of stretch.) A torque wrench applies the correct amount of force and measures it on a dial indicator or calibrated scale. Some even have a disengagement clutch to prevent overapplying torque.

Safety is a prime consideration to the do-it-yourselfer. To protect yourself against accidental injury, use wheel blocks and set the parking brake before starting work. If you're going to work under the car, place it on a sturdy set of jackstands. While these may seem like unnecessary steps, they're safety precautions and safety is never unnecessary, espe-

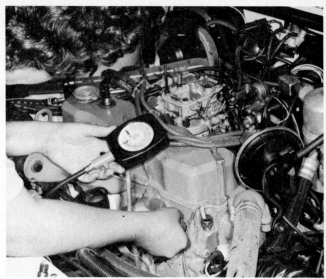

A compression test is one of the best ways to determine engine condition.

cially when there's a distinct possibility that you can hurt yourself. Also, it's a wise idea not to smoke when you're working under the hood—cigarettes and gasoline still do not mix.

Keep a supply of sheetmetal screws handy in case you have to disconnect the fuel line; these can be used as plugs to prevent gas or gas vapors from escaping. If you're not completely at home under the hood, a roll of masking tape and a felt-tipped pen will come in handy. Wrap a piece of tape around each vacuum hose or line you have to disconnect and identify its connection point with the felt-tipped pen.

X-car owners will do well to buy the factory shop manual for their particular year car. It's impossible for us to cover everything relating to the various X-car models within these pages. The more complex the system, the greater the possibility that something will break down and the more difficult it becomes to pinpoint exactly what has gone wrong.

Having the factory shop manual at hand provides you with the most authoritative source of information and data pertaining to your particular car. It also includes many line drawings which can help you visualize the various systems found under the maze of hoses and lines in your engine compartment. To order your own shop manual, refer to the coupon in your owner's handbook or place an order through your dealership's parts department.

To prove our point that it's both easy and fun to do a routine tune-up on your X-car, we've assembled a set of pictorial tune-up sequences for both the 4 and 6-cylinder engines. To keep our tune-up procedures from being redundant, each touches only on the high points.

You should refer to the appropriate chapters for specifics and complete instructions. Even though you may own only one of the engines covered in the tune-up procedures, we strongly suggest you browse through both, since there's useful information that can be applied to your particular circumstances. Now, let's open up the old toolbox and go to work!

Tune-up Specifications

	Engine					Fuel Pump Pressure (PSI)
Year	Displacement (Litres)	VIN Code	Engine Code	Trans.		
1980	2.5	5	WA,WB	Man.		6.5-8.0
	2.5	5	WA,WB	Man.		6.5-8.0
	2.5	5	XA,XB	Auto.		6.5-8.0
	2.5	5	XA,XB	Auto.		6.5-8.0
	2.5	5	WA,WB	Man.		6.5-8.0
	2.5	5	WA,WB	Man.		6.5-8.0
	2.5	5	XA,XB	Auto.		6.5-8.0
	2.5	5	XA,XB	Auto.		6.5-8.0
	2.5	5	A3,AV	Man.		6.5-8.0
	2.5	5	A3,AV	Man.		6.5-8.0
	2.5	5	Z9,Z4,Z6	Auto.		6.5-8.0
	2.5	5	Z9,Z4,Z6	Auto.		6.5-8.0
	2.8	7	CNF,CNH	Man.		6.0-7.5
	2.8	7	CNF,CNH	Man.		6.0-7.5
	2.8	7	CNJ,CNK	Auto.		6.0-7.5
	2.8	7	CNJ,CNK	Auto.		6.0-7.5
	2.8	7	DCZ,DDB	Auto.		6.0-7.5
	2.8	7	DCZ,DDB	Auto.		6.0-7.5
	2.8	7	CNL,CNM	Man.		6.0-7.5
	2.8	7	CNR,CNS	Auto.		6.0-7.5
	2.8	7	CNR,CNS	Auto.		6.0-7.5

	Engine					Type
Year	Displacement (Litres)	VIN Code	Engine Code	Trans.		
1980	2.5	5	WA,WB	Man.		R43TSX
	2.5	5	WA,WB	Man.		R43TSX
	2.5	5	XA,XB	Auto.		R43TSX
	2.5	5	XA,XB	Auto.		R43TSX
	2.5	5	WA,WB	Man.		R43TSX
	2.5	5	WA,WB	Man.		R43TSX
	2.5	5	XA,XB	Auto.		R43TSX
	2.5	5	XA,XB	Auto.		R43TSX
	2.5	5	A3,AV	Man.		R43TSX
	2.5	5	A3,AV	Man.		R43TSX
	2.5	5	Z9,Z4,Z6	Auto.		R43TSX
	2.5	5	Z9,Z4,Z6	Auto.		R43TSX
	2.8	7	CNF,CNH	Man.		R44TS
	2.8	7	CNF,CNH	Man.		R44TS
	2.8	7	CNJ,CNK	Auto.		R44TS
	2.8	7	CNJ,CNK	Auto.		R44TS
	2.8	7	DCZ,DDB	Auto.		R44TS
	2.8	7	DCZ,DDB	Auto.		R44TS
	2.8	7	CNL,CNM	Man.		R44TS
	2.8	7	CNR,CNS	Auto.		R44TS
	2.8	7	CNR,CNS	Auto.		R44TS

Carburetor

Type	Carb. Number	Float Adj.	Initial Timing °BTDC		Idle Speed RPM		Fast Idle RPM
			Man.	Auto.	Man.	Auto.	
2SE	17059617	5.15mm	10	—	1000	—	2400
2SE	17059621	3/16in.	10	—	1000	—	2600
2SE	17059616	5.15mm	—	10	—	650	2600
2SE	17059620	3/16in.	—	10	—	650	2600
2SE	17059615	5.15mm	10	—	1000	—	2400
2SE	17059619	3/16in.	10	—	1000	—	2600
2SE	17059614	5.15mm	—	10	—	650	2600
2SE	17059618	3/16in.	—	10	—	650	2600
E2SE	17059617	11/16in.	10	—	1000	—	2200
E2SE	17059615	11/16in.	10	—	1000	—	2200
E2SE	17059616	11/16in.	—	10	—	650	2600
E2SE	17059614	11/16in.	—	10	—	650	2600
2SE	17059653	3/16in.	2	—	750	—	1900
2SE	17059651	3/16in.	2	—	750	—	1900
2SE	17059652	3/16in.	—	6	—	700	2000
2SE	17059650	3/16in.	—	6	—	700	2000
2SE	17059652	3/16in.	—	6	—	700	2000
2SE	17059650	3/16in.	—	6	—	700	2000
E2SE	17059763	1/8in.	6	—	750	—	2000
E2SE	17059762	1/8in.	—	10	—	700	2000
E2SE	17059760	1/8in.	—	10	—	700	2000

Spark Plug / Distributor

Gap (Ins.)	Torque (Ft.-lbs.)	Model Number	Centrifugal Advance Dist. Degrees @ Dist. RPM		Vacuum Advance Dist. Degrees @ Ins. Hg.	
			Start	Finish	Start	Finish
.060	15	1110783	0@700	10-11.5@2000	0@4	9.5-10@10.5
.060	15	1110783	0@700	10-11.5@2000	0@4	9.5-10@10.5
.060	15	1110783	0@700	10-11.5@2000	0@4	9.5-10@10.5
.060	15	1110783	0@700	10-11.5@2000	0@4	9.5-10@10.5
.060	15	1110782	0@525	10-11.5@2000	0@3.5	8-10.5@8
.060	15	1110782	0@525	10-11.5@2000	0@3.5	8-10.5@8
.060	15	1110782	0@525	10-11.5@2000	0@3.5	8-10.5@8
.060	15	1110782	0@525	10-11.5@2000	0@3.5	8-10.5@8
.060	15	1110787	0@525	11.5@2000	0@3.5	10@9
.060	15	1110787	0@525	11.5@2000	0@3.5	10@9
.060	15	1110786	0@525	9.5-11.5@2000	0@3.5	10.5@9
.060	15	1110786	0@525	9.5-11.5@2000	0@3.5	10.5@9
.045	15	1103362	0@550	12-14@2400	0@3.5	4-6@20
.045	15	1103362	0@550	12-14@2400	0@3.5	4-6@20
.045	15	1103361	0@550	10-12@2400	0@3.5	4-6@20
.045	15	1103361	0@550	10-12@2400	0@3.5	4-6@20
.045	15	1103361	0@550	10-12@2400	0@3.5	4-6@20
.045	15	1103361	0@550	10-12@2400	0@3.5	4-6@20
.045	15	1103362	0@550	12-14@2400	0@3.5	4-6@20
.045	15	1103361	0@550	10-12@2400	0@3.5	4-6@20
.045	15	1103361	0@550	10-12@2400	0@3.5	4-6@20

1. The base engine for all X-cars—the 2.5-litre (151-cubic-inch), 2-barrel L4 engine (RPO LW9)—is built by Pontiac and delivers 90 horsepower (net SAE) at 4000 rpm. Note emissions decal (arrow) for specific information.

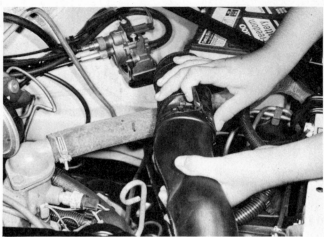

2. Begin by removing the air cleaner. This is a busy-work procedure involving several steps. The first is to unclip the plastic fastener on the zip tube where it connects to the plastic ducting. Work carefully to prevent tearing the zip tube.

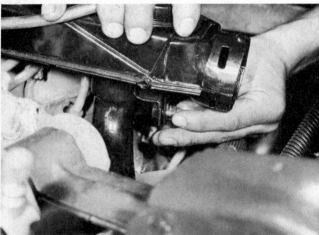

3. Grasp the plastic ducting and pull it off the air cleaner snorkel. A long screw holds snorkel securely to the bracket underneath and must be removed. Don't forget to replace it as it prevents damage from engine vibration.

4. Two cap screws hold the air cleaner in place. Remove screws and lift off the housing cover to check the filter element and crankcase ventilation filter, if used. Wipe inside of housing clean with a solvent-moistened cloth.

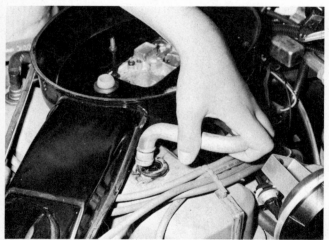

5. To disconnect the air cleaner PCV pipe at the rocker cover, pull upward on the pipe until it pops free of the rubber grommet. Swivel the pipe carefully to one side—it's rather flimsy metal and can be bent easily.

6. Lift the air cleaner housing off the carburetor air horn until it clears the mounting studs, then disconnect the front hose and sensor vacuum line at the rear of the housing. Remove the air cleaner and place it to one side while you work on the engine.

7. The air cleaner gasket is firmly attached to the carburetor air horn. This gasket is designed to prevent an air leak and is important to smooth engine operation. Inspect it carefully for signs of damage or possible leakage points.

8. A bad plug wire will cause an engine misfire, but it can be located quickly with a plug firing indicator. This device hooks under the wire and flashes each time the plug fires. A weak, intermittent, or nonexistent flash means a bad wire.

9. The plugs are in close quarters on the L4 engine and plug cable pliers are a necessity if the engine is warm. Grasp the boot connector with the pliers, twist 45 degrees, and pull up and off plug terminal. Place wire to one side, out of the way.

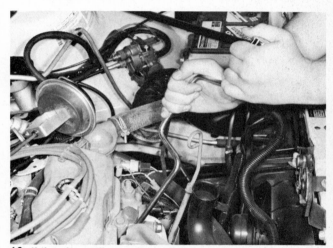

10. If the plug wells are dirty, blow them clean with compressed air or use a parts cleaning brush to remove debris before breaking plugs loose. A speeder wrench and spark plug socket will do the job quickly.

11. A short length of rubber tubing makes a good tool for removing warm plugs from the engine, as well as installing new plugs. Fit the tubing over the plug and use it as a handle to unscrew or screw the plug in place.

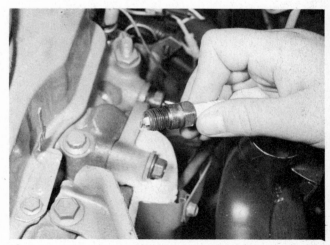

12. A thorough plug inspection gives a good indication of how well the engine is performing. A normal plug will show slight gray or light tan deposits on the tip, with some degree of electrode wear evident.

13. Run a compression test on all cylinders; this gives a good idea of the engine's internal condition. Compare the lowest reading with that of the highest—it should be at least 75 percent of the highest reading.

14. Reinstall plugs finger-tight. If you have a torque wrench, tighten each plug to 15 ft.-lbs. Without a torque wrench, plugs should only be tightened an extra 1/16-turn. If overtightened, plugs may "seize" in the cylinder head.

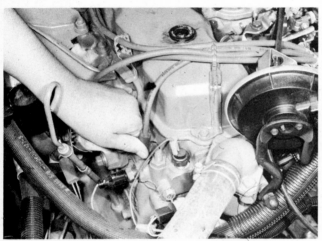

15. Replace the plug wire on the plug terminal by pressing straight down until you feel the connector "click" in place. Make sure the plug wires are properly routed and do not touch each other or rub on accessory units.

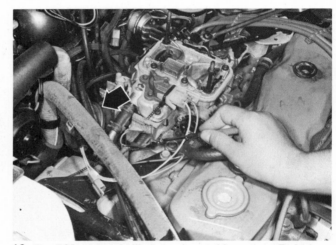

16. The EGR system is likely to give problems (see Emissions chapter, starting on page 76). If hard starting and rough idling develop, check the EGR valve (arrow) before touching the carburetor.

17. In our tune-up, the EGR valve malfunction was traced to excessive carbon deposits which prevented proper valve stem operation and reduced the flow of exhaust gas considerably. A new valve is the answer to our problem.

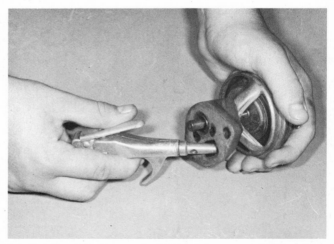

18. Unfortunately, the required EGR valve was on back-order, so we temporarily cleaned the old valve with solvent and a wire brush. Compressed air is used to blow out all debris before replacing the valve on engine.

19. *Remove the PCV valve from the rocker cover. Shake the valve and listen for a rattle or clicking sound inside. Run the engine at idle and hold your finger over the end of the valve. You should feel a vacuum unless the hose or valve is plugged.*

20. *A plugged PCV valve should be replaced with a new one—it cannot be satisfactorily cleaned. An occasional shot of carburetor cleaner, however, will reduce the possibility of the valve plugging up.*

21. *Start the engine and feed the carburetor a can of cleaner. This will reduce the buildup of gum and varnish in the passages. Simple procedures like this can save you dollars in carburetor overhauls.*

22. *A pressure test will tell you if the fuel pump is delivering as it should. "T" the pressure gauge into the fuel line between the carburetor and fuel pump, then check the reading at idle against the specifications.*

23. *The choke pull-down mechanism can be tested with a hand vacuum pump. Connect the vacuum pump to the diaphragm; as you draw a vacuum, the linkage should move. The diaphragm has a bleeder hole and will not hold a vacuum.*

24. *Connect a tachometer and start the engine. (Make sure the tach is set on 4-cylinder setting.) Let the engine warm to normal operating temperature, and compare the idle speed to specifications. If an adjustment is called for, follow the directions on the emissions decal.*

25. Turn the idle speed screw to set curb idle to specifications. Place the fast idle screw (arrow) on the highest step of the fast idle cam and adjust the screw in or out as necessary to obtain specified fast idle speed.

26. Air conditioned cars require a second idle speed adjustment. Open the throttle slightly to allow the solenoid plunger to extend fully, then turn the solenoid adjusting screw to set the idle to the specified rpm.

27. Before replacing the air cleaner housing, pry off the clip holding the PCV filter pack inside housing. Not all air cleaners are fitted with this device, so don't worry if yours happens to be one of those without it.

28. Don't try to clean the filter pack; replace it with a new one. It's a good idea to install a new air cleaner filter and PCV element at the same time. Fit the new pack in place and reinstall the clamp on the outside of the housing.

29. Connect vacuum lines under the air cleaner, place the air cleaner on the carburetor air horn, and press the PCV tube into rocker cover. Reinstall the snorkel screw, fit the plastic duct in place, and connect it to the zip tube. Install a new filter and replace the cover.

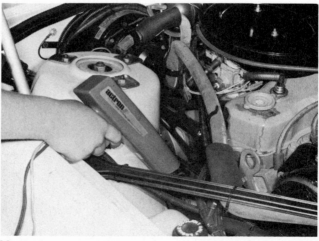

30. Hook up your timing light, start the engine, and check the timing. Under normal circumstances, no adjustment should be necessary, but if it is, the distributor is located at rear of the engine under the manifold. Your engine should now be running perfectly.

1. The 173-cubic-inch (2.8L) V6 manufactured by Chevrolet is an optional X-car engine. Our tune-up car is a 1980 Federal version (without C-4) equippd with a manual transaxle.

2. The V6 air cleaner uses a single wing nut. Remove the nut and cover, disconnect the fresh air tube, and pull the metal tubes from the Pulsair valves (front and rear) to remove the housing.

3. Plug cable pliers are as necessary to remove cables as on L4, but are more difficult to use here. The rear bank cables and plugs require working blind and a lot patience.

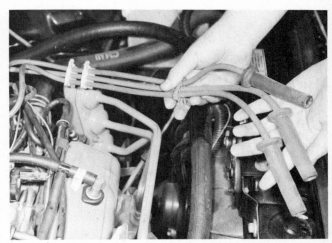

4. Wipe the plug cables clean and inspect condition of insulation. Proper cable routing will extend their life, so be sure to reconnect wire looms properly.

5. A speeder wrench with 90-degree angle extension works well to remove plugs on front bank. The remaining three plugs are more difficult and time-consuming to remove/install.

6. Inspect plug condition. The one shown here has a bent side electrode, closing the spark gap completely. Little wonder the engine misfired.

7. *Run a compression test with the plugs out. Disable the HEI distributor and crank the engine over four to six times to build up compression reading. Lowest cylinder reading should be 75 percent of the highest.*

8. *Reinstall the plugs finger-tight, then tighten an extra 1/16th turn using the speeder. Replace the cables and make sure each seats fully on the plug terminal.*

9. *Disconnect the distributor vacuum advance diaphragm hose and connect a hand vacuum pump. Draw 8-10 inches of vacuum to test diaphragm operation.*

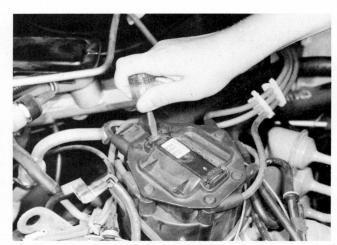

10. *To service the distributor or replace the spark plug cables, depress the latches on opposite ends of the cap as shown. This frees the plug wire loom from cap.*

11. *Remove plug cable loom by lifting straight up and off distributor cap. Individual cables can be replaced at this point if necessary by popping them out of the loom.*

12. *Four screws hold the distributor cap to the housing. To remove cap, press down on each screw with a screwdriver and rotate 90 degrees. Screw will turn in only one direction.*

13. Lift the cap up and off distributor housing. Wipe inside of cap with a clean paper towel and inspect for hairline cracks, burned contacts, or other defects.

14. The HEI distributor rotor is held in place by two screws. Loosen screws and remove the rotor. Inspect the rotor for defects.

15. Check the centrifugal advance action by moving the cam to one side and pulling advance weights apart. Let go and watch the motion as weights return. If sluggish, mechanism needs cleaning.

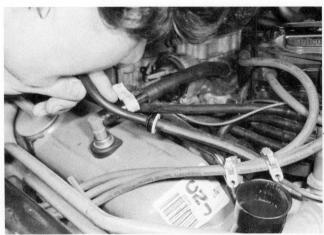

16. Check-valves can be tested by mouth suction. Valve should pass vacuum in only one direction. If removed from vacuum line, be sure to replace it correctly.

17. The EGR valve is located to the left of the carburetor and mounts directly to the intake manifold without use of a spacer plate. Mirror is handy to watch valve stem action.

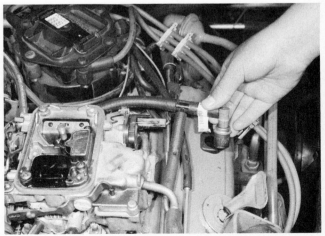

18. Check PCV valve by pulling it out of rocker arm cover and shaking. You should hear a clicking sound when shaken if the valve condition is satisfactory for reuse. If not, install a new PCV valve.

19. A PCV system tester can be used on the valve cover, but a piece of medium weight paper will work as well. If suction holds the paper in place with the engine running, the system is O.K.

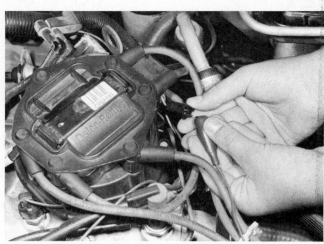

20. An extension tachometer connector is provided to hook up an engine tach for carburetor adjustment/timing. The newer inductive tachs can be used without this connection.

21. It doesn't matter what kind of tach you use, as long as it's accurate. This Cal Custom/Hawk Pocketune is a small, self-contained unit you can carry with you.

22. Check operation of choke butterfly by pushing linkage as shown. The linkage should operate smoothly without binding. Make sure it stays this way with a shot of WD-40.

23. Start engine and spray a can of carb cleaner into the venturi. This will clean the internal passages and reduce the possibility of a carburetor overhaul down the road.

24. Install a new fuel filter. (Refer to Fuel Systems chapter for a better view.) Use a 15/16-inch wrench to hold the inlet fitting while breaking the connection loose with a second wrench.

25. If fuel problems seem apparent, "T" a pressure gauge into the fuel line and run a pressure test on the fuel pump to see if it's up to specs.

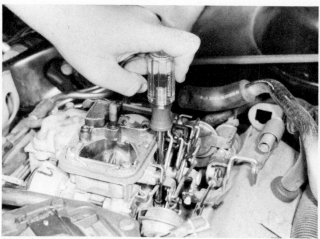

26. The curb idle screw is located under all this linkage at the rear of the carburetor. Set the idle to decal specs. The mixture needle is sealed and cannot be adjusted.

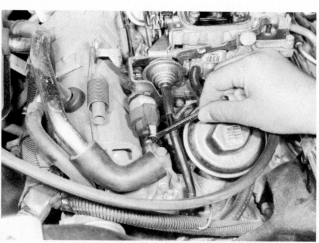

27. Open the throttle enough to extend the solenoid plunger, then turn the solenoid screw to adjust the idle to specified rpm. Reconnect the solenoid electrical lead after adjustment.

28. Reaching the fast idle screw can be a chore. To set fast idle speed, make sure the screw is on the specified cam step and turn the screw until correct rpm is reached.

29. Wipe inside of air cleaner housing with a clean cloth moistened in solvent. Reinstall the air cleaner on engine, drop in a clean air filter element, and button it up.

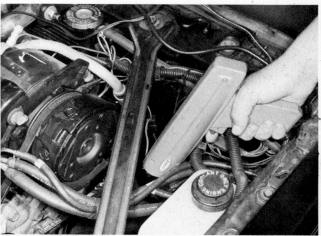

30. Connect a timing light and take a look at the ignition timing. If an adjustment is necessary, loosen the distributor hold-down, rotate distributor to align timing marks, and tighten.

4

Starting and Charging

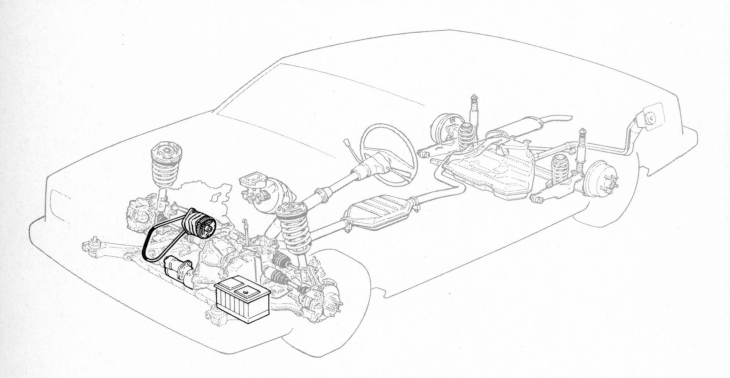

The battery is an integral part of any car's electrical system. It's also responsible for most starting and charging problems you'll encounter. To keep such problems to a minimum, it is important that you service the battery regularly and keep it in good shape. All X-cars are factory-equipped with the Delco Freedom battery.

The Delco Freedom battery is a sealed unit with a small vent hole in one side at the top of the case. This vent allows any gas produced in the battery to escape, preventing the buildup of internal pressure. The Freedom battery requires, and will accept, *no water* during its life. It also has built-in overcharge protection. When an excessive voltage level is applied to the Freedom battery, it will not accept as much current as a conventional battery.

Look at the top of the battery case and you'll see a small circular charge indicator ''eye.'' This is really a temperature-corrected hydrometer built into the battery. It allows you to check the state of charge visually. Wipe the top of the eye clean and look straight down at it. If a green dot is visible in the center of the eye, the battery is normal. When the eye appears dark and no green dot can be seen, the battery should be charged and tested. The eye will appear clear or light yellow in color if the battery has failed. When this condition is noted, do not try to charge, test, or jump-start the battery—replace it.

You can't test a Freedom battery with hydrometers, battery cell indicators, or other conventional test equipment. A load test is the only practical way to determine how healthy the battery is, and to perform this test, you'll need a voltmeter and a load tester. The voltmeter is a piece of test equipment you should have handy; the load tester is far more specialized so it's not likely you'll own one. However, you may be able to borrow one or have the test performed at a garage. Here's how it's done.

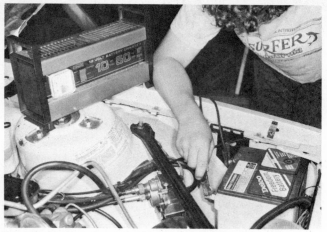
Proper starting/charging system care begins with a fully charged battery.

Disconnect the ignition wire harness at the HEI distributor and crank the engine for about 15 seconds. This will remove any surface charge from the battery. Now connect the voltmeter and load tester and apply the following load according to the battery type installed in your car: 85-60, 170 amps; 87-60, 210 amps; 89-60, 230 amps. You'll find the battery type on the label. Hold the load for 15 seconds, read the voltmeter, and remove the load. Estimate the outside temperature and compare your voltmeter reading to that specified in Table 1.

Table 1

Estimated Temperature (Degrees)	Minimum Voltage
70 F. (21 C.)	9.6
50 F. (10 C.)	9.4
30 F. (0 C.)	9.1
15 F. (−10 C.)	8.8
0 F. (−18 C.)	8.5
0 F. (Below: −18 C.)	8.0

Since the Freedom battery has no vent caps, you should have little problem with corrosion. Yet it's still a good idea to wipe the battery top clean during your weekly inspection. Every six months, disconnect the battery cable terminals and give them a thorough cleaning. If corrosion is allowed to form, it will eventually attack the battery cables. Corroded cable strands reduce the current from the battery to the starter, and the greater load placed on the good part of the cable will cause it to overheat during current flow. Overheating increases resistance in the cable, which further reduces current flow.

Should you find it necessary to jump-start an X-car because of a dead battery, there are some precautions you should take. Check the charge indicator eye first—if it's clear or light yellow, do not try to jump-start it. The battery may explode under such circumstances, causing serious personal injury.

If the eye indicates that jump-starting is okay (green or dark), connect one end of the positive jumper cable to the positive terminal of the good battery and connect the other end to the positive terminal of the dead battery. Hook one end of the negative jumper cable to the negative terminal of the good battery and connect the other end to a good *engine ground* away from the battery. This will prevent the possibility of the dead battery exploding

Fuses and Circuit Breakers

The electrical circuits in your X-car are protected from shorts by a combination of fuses, circuit breakers, and fusible links in the wiring circuits. The fuse box is located under the instrument panel on the passenger side.

A circuit breaker in the light switch protects the headlight wiring. The windshield wiper motor is protected by a fuse and a circuit breaker. X-cars equipped with power windows and power door locks have separate circuit breakers located on the engine compartment bulkhead.

Fuse requirements for other circuits are listed below. You should carry an assortment of spare fuses in the car.

CIRCUIT	RATING
Radio	10 Amp.
Idle Stop Solenoid and Pulse Wiper	10 Amp.
Wiper	25 Amp.
Stop, Rear & Front, Hazard Lamps, I.P. Indicators	20 Amp.
Dir. Sig., B.U. Lamps	20 Amp.
Heater, A/C	25 Amp.
Inst. Lamps, Radio Dial Lamp, Heater Dial Lamp, W/S Wiper Lamp, Cigarette Lighter & Ash Tray	4 Amp.
Gauges Warning Lamps, Cruise Control, Brake Alarm, Oil, Rear Defogger, Fuel Gauge, Headlight Buzzer, Seat Belt Warning Buzzer, Temp., Gen.	10 Amp.
Glove Box Lamp, Dome Lamp, Luggage Lamp, Clock, Hood, Lighter, Courtesy Lamps, Key Warning	20 Amp.
Tail, Parking and Side Marker Lamps, License Lamp	20 Amp.

Do not use fuses of higher amperage rating than those recommended above.

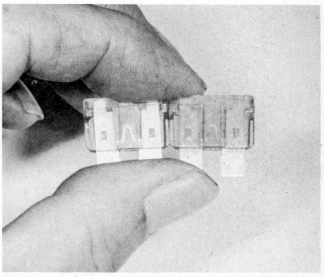
All X-cars use the new blade-type fuses. The one at the left is good, as shown by the metal connection between the blades. The blown fuse at the right shows a broken connection.

from the sudden surge of electricity provided by the good battery.

Start the car with the good battery first; then start the one with the dead battery. *Do not* rev the engine after starting, but let it return to a normal idle. To disconnect the jumper leads properly, reverse the connection procedure exactly. The negative cable should be removed from the engine ground first.

The X-car starting system includes the battery, the starter or cranking motor, a solenoid (mounted on top of the motor), the ignition switch, and related circuit wiring. In addition, manual transmission cars have a clutch start switch located on the clutch pedal lever support which closes when the pedal is depressed, allowing current to flow. Cars fitted with an automatic transmission use a neutral safety switch which permits starting the engine only when the selector lever is in the Park or Neutral position.

To see your starter this clearly, you'll have to pull the radiator. Note the end bracket and the slip-on nylon connection protector at the solenoid.

Watch this point (arrow) of the battery ground cable. Terminal corrosion can cause problems here.

When the ignition switch is turned to Start, the starter engages the engine flywheel and spins the engine fast enough to start it. Heavy cables, connectors, and switches are used because of the considerable current required by the starter when the engine is cranked. The starter solenoid is a separate sealed unit mounted on the starter and connected to the starter field by a metal strap. X-cars use a Delco 5MT starter which is essentially the same as other GM starters except that the field coils are permanently mounted to the motor frame.

Testing the starting system is simple. If you suspect that something is wrong, turn on the headlights and try to start the engine. If the lights go out, look for a poor connection between the starter and

battery. Broken or corroded cables and terminals will cause this condition. If the lights simply dim while the starter cranks slowly, there's a drag on the engine which is making the starter work too hard. Should the lights stay bright but the starter doesn't turn over, the trouble may be in the wiring, ignition switch, or inside the starter itself.

To eliminate the wiring and ignition switch as possibilities, make a temporary contact between the large battery terminal on the starter solenoid and the smaller terminal connected to the ignition switch. Use a screwdriver to make the connection and make sure the transmission is either in Neutral or Park. If the starter works now when you turn the key, the trouble has to be in the wiring or ignition switch.

Test the neutral safety switch on X-cars with an automatic transmission next. Locate the switch at the bottom of the steering column and bypass it with a jumper wire. Place the transmission selector lever in Neutral and try the ignition switch. If the starter works, the problem is a defective neutral safety switch.

Should the starter fail to work under any of the circumstances above, connect a heavy booster cable directly from the battery's hot side to the terminal on the starter. If the starter still doesn't run, the problem is inside the starter; if it does turn over, the solenoid is faulty.

If the solenoid makes a clicking sound when the key is turned to Start and the starter doesn't run but will run with the booster cable connected, the solenoid is not necessarily good. The internal contacts may be burned enough to prevent the solenoid from switching on the heavy starter current. The solenoid used with the 5MT cannot be repaired—it must be replaced with a new one.

A voltmeter will do a more accurate job of checking out the starting system. Start by checking cranking voltage. Connect the voltmeter to the battery in correct polarity and crank the engine with the HEI distributor disconnected. Battery voltage should not fall below 9.0 volts. While the engine is cranking, check the cranking speed. This can be done by ear or with a tachometer. Cranking speed should be at least 180 rpm if the system is operating properly.

If the starter motor runs normally when the key is

X-Car Starting System

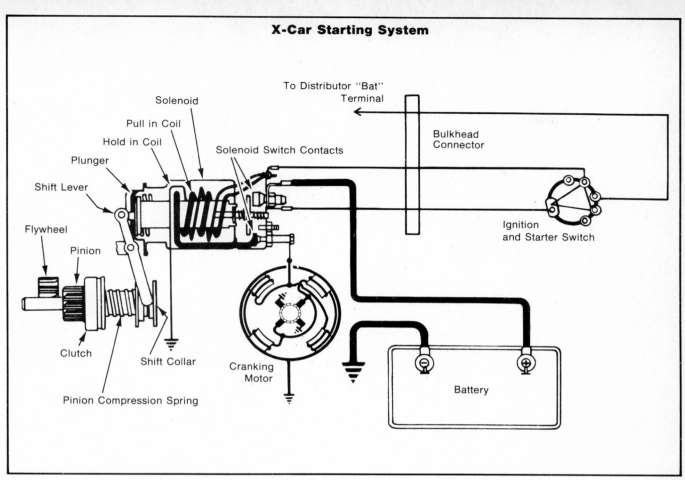

X-Car Charging System

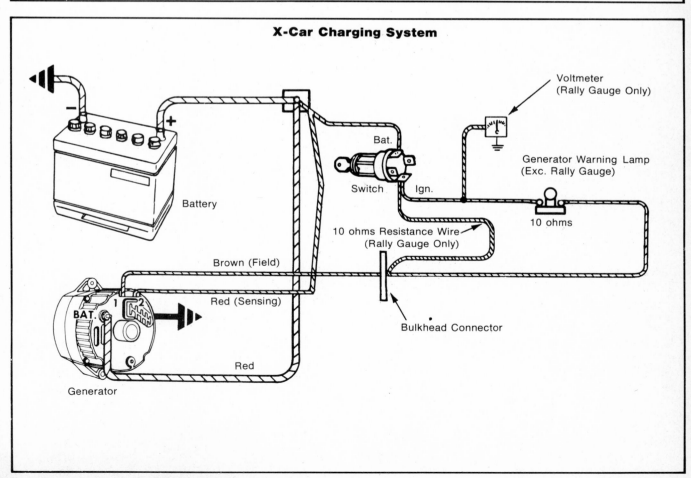

turned to Start, but the engine doesn't crank over, something is wrong with the drive mechanism. The pad-mounted 5MT starter used on X-cars may have a shim between the starter and the engine block. The shim determines the exact mesh of the pinion teeth with the flywheel. If you remove the starter for any reason, be sure to replace it with the same shim. When installing a different starter (new or rebuilt), you should check the pinion teeth-to-ring gear clearance on the old starter before removing it, and then make sure to shim the replacement to obtain the same clearance.

Slip off the nylon protector and disconnect the solenoid leads.

First, disconnect the battery ground cable from the battery. To remove the starter, begin with this bracket.

The X-car charging system includes the battery, a Delcotron alternator, the ignition switch, and connecting wiring. To protect the Delcotron's diode trio, a 10-ohm resistance is provided by the warning light or a resistance wire used with models which have the optional voltmeter. Two models of the Delcotron are used on the X-car: the 15-SI on air-conditioned models and the 10-SI on all others. Internally, the two alternators are identical except that the 15-SI uses delta stator windings and the stator cannot be checked for opens.

The most common charging system problem is a lack of charge, indicated to the driver by the flicker or constant glow of the indicator lamp while the engine is running. This condition is usually caused by a loose or broken fan belt. If you check belt tension and condition regularly, there should be few charging system problems, as long as you maintain the battery properly.

Carry a spare fan belt and a wrench in the car just in case emergency repairs are necessary on the road. Since the alternator drive belt is positioned on the rear pulley, you'll have to loosen the mounting bolts of the accessory units whose drive belts are forward of the alternator belt. Slip each of these belts off and install the alternator belt around the crankshaft pulley and over the alternator pulley. Carefully pry the alternator away from the engine block and tighten the adjusting bolt. Press down on the center of the belt between the two pulleys with your finger, and the belt should deflect approxi-

mately ⅜ inch. If not, loosen the adjusting bolt and move the alternator in the proper direction until belt deflection is correct. Snug the adjusting bolt down tightly.

Replace each of the other accessory belts in their correct order and pry the accessory units away from the engine block, tightening the adjusting bolt. Check belt tension as you did with the alternator belt, and snug the adjusting bolt down tightly on each unit.

If a problem not related to a loose belt or weak battery develops, you can troubleshoot it with the following procedure. Begin by checking the indicator lamp on the instrument panel. If it's working properly, it should come on only when the ignition is on and the engine is not running.

If the light remains on with the ignition off, disconnect the 1 and 2 terminals at the alternator. The lamp will remain on if there is a short between these two leads or go off if there is a problem inside the Delcotron.

If the lamp does not come on when the ignition is on (engine not running), connect a voltmeter between the alternator 2 terminal and ground. A no-voltage reading tells you there is an open circuit between the terminal and the battery. If a voltage reading is shown, disconnect both the 1 and 2 leads from the alternator and momentarily ground the 1

The bracket at the rear of the starter comes off next.

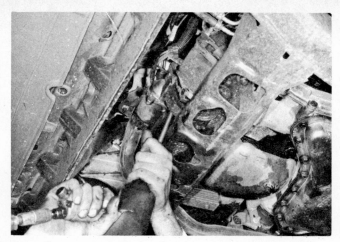
The pad-mounted starter housing is held to the engine by two bolts. Remove the front one.

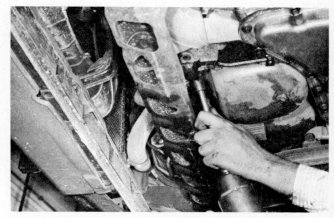
The other starter bolt is reached from behind the splash shield.

The starter can now be disengaged from the flywheel and removed. Be careful—it's heavier than it looks.

Remove the bracket and install it on the new starter. Reverse the steps to replace the starter on the car.

lead. If the lamp does not light now, there's either an open in the 1 circuit, a blown-out fuse, or the indicator bulb has burned out. If the lamp does light with the 1 lead grounded, reconnect both leads to the alternator and move on to the procedure below.

Insert a screwdriver blade inside the ground test hole at the right of the rear face of the alternator and ground the tab inside to the alternator body. This grounds the winding, so if the lamp doesn't light, you know that there's a problem internally. It could be bad brushes, a faulty field winding, or worn slip rings. If the lamp does light, the tiny transistorized regulator inside the alternator is defective. The regulator cannot be adjusted and must be replaced once the alternator has been disassembled.

This test can be performed on the V6 engine without too much difficulty, but space is limited around the rear of the L4 engine, so you'll have to work blindly with a small screwdriver. You should only insert the screwdriver blade about ¾ inch to ground the winding; inserting it further can cause damage to internal components.

Fusible links are used with both the starting and charging circuits to protect them against electrical shorts to ground in the wiring harness, or a heavy current flow. A fusible link is a short piece of wire covered with a special high-temperature insulation. Several sizes smaller than the circuit wiring which it supplies with power, the fusible link will melt when shorted or fed excessive current.

The starting circuit is protected by a single fusible link located at the starter solenoid connection. Three links protect the charging circuit—two at the starter solenoid connections and one at a connector on the right-hand cowl. To replace a damaged fusible link, cut it out of the circuit wiring and splice in a new link of the same capacity.

On the following pages, we've provided a photo sequence showing how the 5MT starter and 10-SI alternator are disassembled. You may wish to simply replace a defective starter/alternator with a rebuilt unit rather than trouble yourself with disassembling and testing yours, but even if this is the case, the step-by-step sequences will give you an excellent idea of what's inside the units and how

Starting and Charging-Battery Care

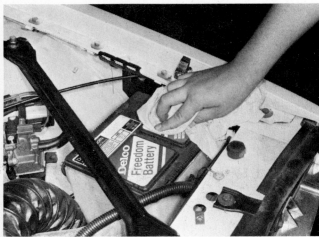

1. Battery case care is important. Check the case for cracks, and wipe it off periodically to remove any surface dust and acid that can form a conductive charge.

2. You may need a flashlight to check the built-in hydrometer. A green dot in the center of the eye indicates a good battery; replace it if the center is clear or yellow.

3. For access to the battery and its side terminals, disconnect the fresh air duct tubing, remove the crosspiece bolt, and swing the crosspiece to one side.

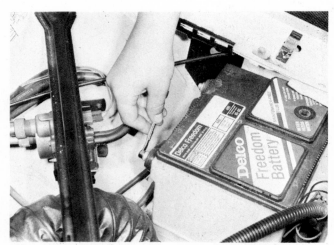

4. A 7mm wrench is used to remove or tighten the side-mounted terminals. Do not overtighten them or you may cause internal damage to the battery.

5. After removing the cable clamps from the battery terminals, clean the battery connection to remove any corrosion. A side-terminal cleaning brush does the job easily.

6. The reverse end of the terminal brush is used to clean the cable connection. When the connector is bright and shiny, you'll have a good electrical connection.

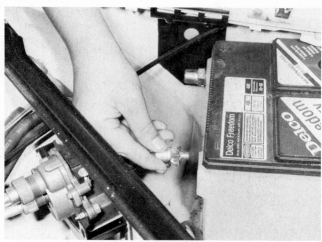

7. If the battery requires charging, you should have a set of screw-in battery posts. These inexpensive accessories provide a good conductive surface for the charger leads.

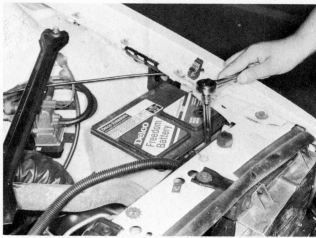

8. The battery hold-down is at the front of the battery case and requires the use of a 12 to 14-inch socket extension. You'll have to work almost by feel at this point.

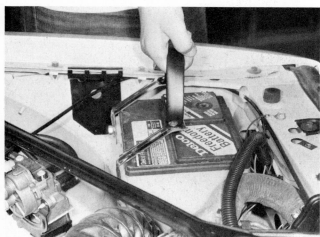

9. This inexpensive battery strap screws into the side terminals and equalizes weight on the strap for easy, safe battery removal. Batteries are heavier than they look, so play it safe.

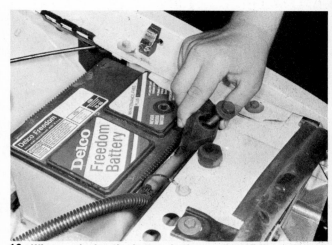

10. When replacing the battery in the car, install the hold-down block by hand and thread the bolt into the carrier hole; then, run it down snugly with the socket extension.

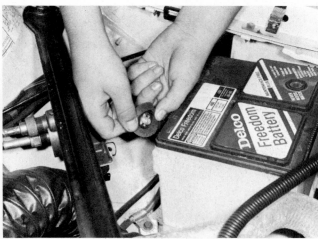

11. Corrosion-preventive-impregnated pads are not as messy as battery sprays. Use a set on the cable connectors to inhibit corrosion and prolong battery life.

12. After making sure the battery is snugly in place and the connections are secure, reinstall the crosspiece bolt and reconnect the fresh-air ducting.

Starting and Charging-Starter Overhaul

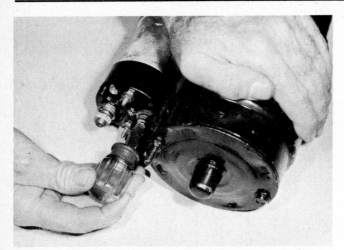

1. Remove the screw connecting the solenoid motor terminal to the field coil connector and begin disassembly of the Delco-Remy 5MT starting motor.

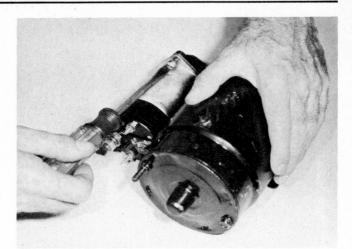

2. The 5MT starter is virtually identical to the 10MT used on other GM cars, except for the permanent field coils. Remove the solenoid attaching screws.

3. Withdraw the solenoid carefully. The plunger spring inside the housing exerts a good deal of pressure and can send the solenoid unit flying across the room.

4. This is the spring to be cautious about. Note that it is the same at both ends. Remove from the solenoid plunger and place to one side for reassembly.

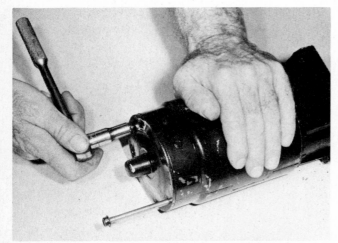

5. With the solenoid removed from the starter housing, loosen and remove the two through-bolts from the end plate. An end plate bracket is also used to fasten the starter in place.

6. The end plate will now slip off easily. Note the leather washer on the end of the armature shaft. Check the end plate bushing carefully for wear or damage.

7. Twist the housing components slightly and remove the commutator end frame, the field frame, and the armature assembly from the drive housing.

8. The commutator brushes are retained in the brush holder by two screws. If the brushes are pitted or worn more than half their original length, install new ones.

9. Don't mistakenly pull the brush holder pivot pin out to remove the brushes, or you'll end up with a mess like this. Everything falls out once the pivot pin is removed.

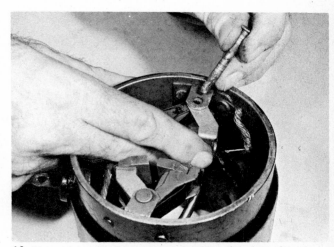

10. If you do make the mistake of pulling the pivot pin, use the other brush holder assembly as a guide to help you position the pieces correctly while replacing the pivot pin.

11. If the shift fork is not to be removed, angle the armature shaft to disengage the drive gear pulley from the fork legs and remove the armature shaft from the drive housing.

12. On some Delco-Remy starters, the shift-fork pivot pin can simply be driven out for removal, but this particular one uses a snap ring (arrow) to hold the pivot pin in place.

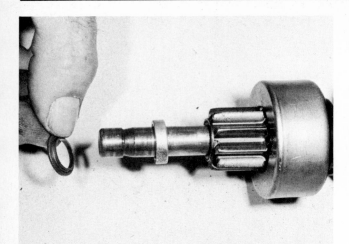

13. *Before the snap ring and retaining ring holding the drive mechanism on the shaft can be removed, you should separate this lip seal ring from the front of the retainer.*

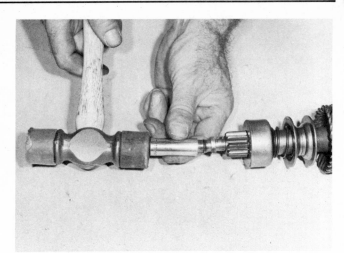

14. *For drive mechanism removal, use a socket and mallet as shown to drive the retaining ring back off the snap ring. Tap gently and do not put the armature in a vise for this step.*

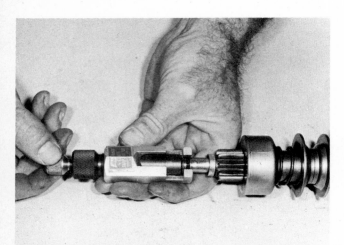

15. *A starter snap ring removal tool such as this expedites removal of the snap ring. Simply screw it in place and rotate the second screw to force the ring up and out of the groove.*

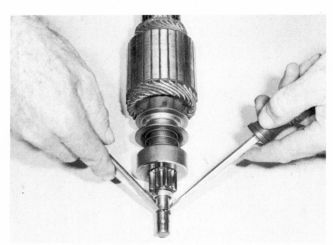

16. *Without a snap ring remover tool, you'll have to pry the snap ring from its groove with two pliers as shown. Snap-ring pliers will not do the job in this case.*

17. *Once the snap ring has been removed, the drive mechanism can be withdrawn from the armature shaft. Check the shaft splines for wear or damage; then inspect the drive mechanism.*

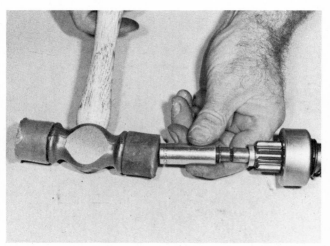

18. *A new snap ring should be installed when replacing the drive mechanism on the armature shaft. Fit the snap ring to the end of the shaft and force it in place with a socket.*

19. If the starter solenoid is not operating properly, it can be easily disassembled and the contact washer checked. Remove the holding screws and take the nuts off the terminals.

20. Remove the solenoid cover. The plunger assembly cannot be disassembled. If the contact ring is worn or corroded, the plunger assembly must be replaced as a unit.

21. To reinstall the starter drive in the housing without removing the shift fork, angle the shaft (arrow) so that it bypasses the housing bushing and connect the fork to the pulley.

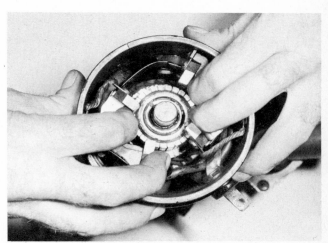

22. You must hold all four brushes against the field frame with your fingers to install the armature. Work slowly and do not try to force the armature in place.

23. If you remove and replace the commutator brushes, their contour must match that of the armature. The arrows point to "incorrectly" installed brushes; unscrew and reverse them.

24. Fit the drive housing and field frame together; then reconnect the field coil and solenoid motor terminal. Replace the end frame and install the through-bolts to complete the overhaul.

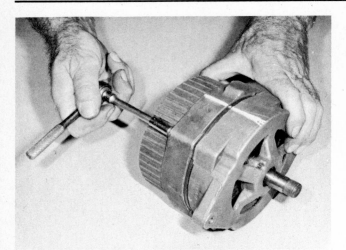

1. Very dependable, this model Delcotron has been used on GM cars for a decade. Begin overhaul by scribing a reference mark across the end frames and remove the through-bolts.

2. The slip-ring end frame and stator should separate from the rotor end frame easily. If they don't, pry them apart carefully, using a screwdriver at each side of the stator slot provided.

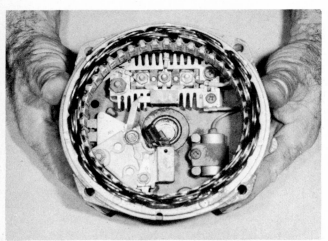

3. It looks fairly complicated inside, but this is really one of the easiest alternators to work on. Use this photo as a reference when you complete reassembly to check your work.

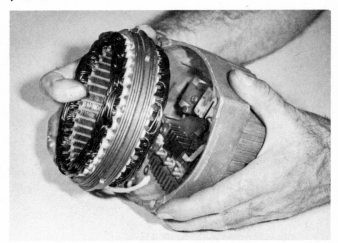

4. Remove the three nuts which hold the stator leads to the heat sink; then lift the stator off the end frame and place to one side on a solid surface for testing.

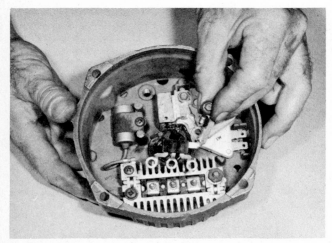

5. Remove the screw holding the diode trio to the brush holder assembly; then remove the trio from the end frame. The diode trio can be checked for a grounded bush lead clip at this time.

6. Disconnect the capacitor lead from the heat sink, and then unscrew and remove the capacitor. The capacitor should be tested before it is reinstalled in the end frame.

7. Now remove the rectifier bridge attaching screw and the BAT terminal screw, lifting the rectifier bridge from the end frame. Keep track of the different screws as you remove them.

8. Remove the two attaching screws holding the brush holder and integral voltage regulator assembly. Two insulators are assembled over the top of the brush retaining clips; the screws have sleeves.

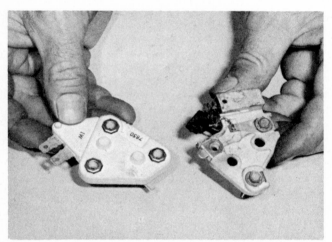

9. Separate the voltage regulator from the brush holder. Remove the brush springs and set them aside. Inspect the brushes for excessive wear, and replace if necessary. Always replace in pairs.

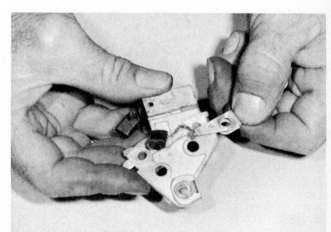

10. Both brush assemblies are identical and simply slip off the holder. Brush leads are connected to the brush assemblies, and the entire unit is replaced by slipping a new one in place.

11. Test the stator for ground by touching one lead of a test lamp or ohmmeter to the stator frame and the other lead to a stator lead. If the lamp lights or ohmmeter reads low, discard the stator.

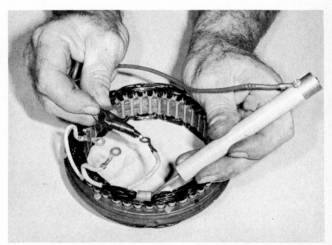

12. Test the stator for opens; the lamp will light or ohmmeter will read low. If that's the case, discard the stator.

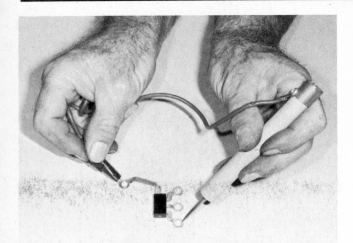

13. To test the diode trio, connect one test lamp lead to the single connector and the other lead to any one of the three connectors, and note whether or not the lamp lights.

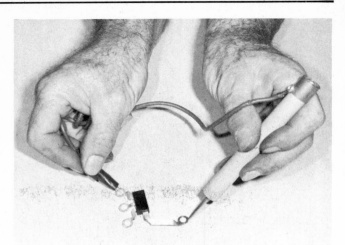

14. Reverse the test leads on the same connectors and note lamp reaction. The test lamp should light in one direction only if the diode trio is good. If it lights in both cases or does not light, replace the trio.

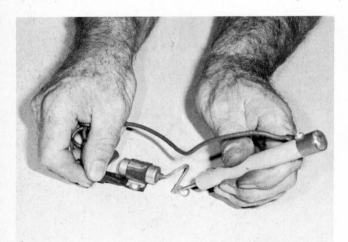

15. The capacitor can also be tested with the same test lamp. It should not light if the unit is satisfactory. If the lamp does light, the capacitor is shorted and should be replaced.

16. Check the rotor for an open by touching each test lead to the slip rings as shown. The test lamp will light if the windings are okay. An ohmmeter can be used; it should give a high reading.

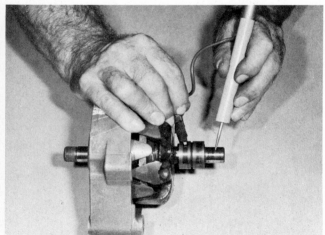

17. To test the rotor for grounds, connect the test lamp leads as shown. If the ground is good, the lamp should light. If rotor slip rings require cleaning, use a fine polishing cloth and blow dry to remove any residue.

18. Begin the Delcotron reassembly by reinstalling the voltage regulator and brush holder. The regulator slips into position in the end frame holder; two holes in the brush holder fit over the regulator studs.

19. Before replacing the brush holder attaching screws, check the insulating sleeve on each; be sure they're not cracked or damaged. The screw shown here may or may not have an insulating washer.

20. Install the brush springs and fit the brushes in the holder; then insert a small drill bit or piece of stiff wire through a hole in the end frame (arrow) to keep the brushes in place.

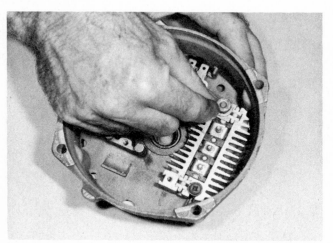

21. Install the BAT terminal from the rear, with the fit rectifier bridge over it, and install the retaining screw with insulator at the other end. Replace the nut on the BAT terminal, which holds the left side of the bridge.

22. Reinstall the capacitor, connect its lead to the rectifier bridge, and then replace the diode trio. The trio attaching screw must have an insulating sleeve. The trio leads fit over the rectifier bridge terminals.

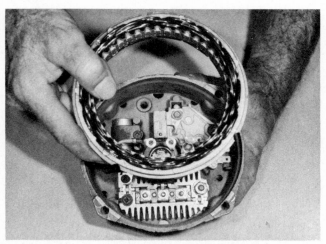

23. The stator is the final part to be replaced. Fit its leads over the rectifier bridge terminals and seat the stator; then replace the terminal attaching nuts.

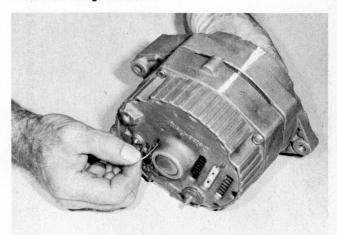

24. Align the end frames according to your scribed mark, fit together, and install the through-bolts. Remove the drill bit or wire to allow the brushes to contact slip rings. The overhaul is complete.

5

The Ignition System

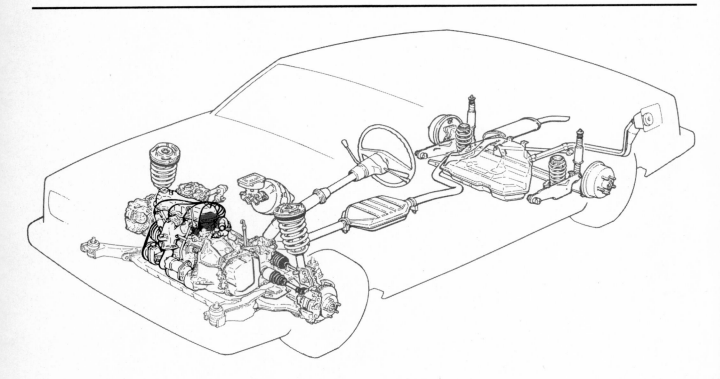

The X-car ignition system includes the battery, an HEI distributor, the ignition switch, four or six spark plugs, and the primary/secondary wiring. All other ignition components are contained within the HEI (High Energy Ignition) distributor. The ignition coil is located underneath a cover in the distributor cap. Inside the distributor body, you'll find a permanent magnet, a pole piece and timer core with teeth, and a pickup coil. These replace the conventional breaker points and condenser used on all cars before 1975.

How it Works

The timer core rotates inside the pole piece. When its teeth align with those on the pole piece, it causes an induced voltage in the pickup coil to signal the electronic module, which is also located inside the distributor body. The brains of

the ignition system, this module triggers the coil to send its secondary voltage to the plug wires according to the relative position of the timer core/ pole piece teeth. As long as the module operates properly, the HEI distributor is highly reliable, requiring little service beyond a periodic check of the vacuum and centrifugal advance mechanism.

The centrifugal advance changes the position of the timer core relative to the distributor shaft. This is done by two governor weights held close together at the top of the distributor shaft by small springs. As the shaft's rotational speed increases, the weights tend to fly apart, stretching the springs. The further they allow the weights to fly outward, the further the timer core position (and thus spark timing) will be advanced. The precisely calibrated tension of the springs is thus the primary controlling factor in the operation of the centrifugal advance mechanism.

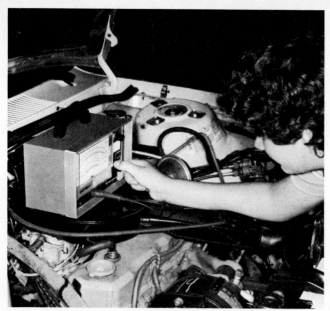

An electronic ignition analyzer such as this Actron unit will help you troubleshoot the HEI ignition.

The 4-cylinder engine's distributor is located on the rear of the engine, close to the firewall. In theory, it is removable, but in practice, you'll find it impossible to service even the plug wires without lifting the entire engine about 14 inches out of the engine compartment. If GM shops find it necessary to do this (and they do), so will you.

The V6 distributor is positioned in the valley between the engine heads to the right of the carburetor. This can be more easily serviced than the L4 distributor, but you'll find it easier to work on if you remove the air cleaner housing. Such compact packaging has made it necessary to run a pigtail lead from the distributor cap tachometer (TACH) terminal for ease in connecting test instruments. Do not try to hook directly to the distributor cap terminal—use the pigtail instead.

Proper distributor cap sealing is important. Hairline cracks or chips will allow dirt and moisture to enter the distributor housing. It's a good idea to periodically remove the cap and check it for cracks or excessive wear/corrosion of the terminals inside. Carbon tracks between the terminals will cause electrical leakage. You should also carefully remove the plug wires from the cap towers and check the terminals for corrosion or burning. HEI cap tower terminals look much like spark plug terminals, as they do not use the older push-in type connections. This produces a firmer connection and makes them easier to clean. Use a wire brush to resurface the terminals before replacing the plug wires. This is also a good time to remove the rotor and inspect it for cracks, excessive burning, or corrosion.

If you find it necessary to remove the coil from the cap, you'll find a large rubber seal under the coil. This seal absorbs moisture and prevents shorting. If it is no longer flexible, replace it with a new one. There's also a small spring on the cap contact button which fits inside the seal. Be sure to replace this spring or you'll have an open circuit between the cap button and the coil secondary contact.

A vacuum diaphragm connected to the magnetic pickup assembly by a linkage arm controls vacuum advance. When there is vacuum in the chamber of the advance unit, air pressure deflects the diaphragm against its spring loading, and the linkage advances the spark timing by rotating the pickup. When the vacuum drops, the diaphragm is not deflected as much, retarding the spark slightly. Vacuum is provided from a carburetor port above or below the throttle valves.

Testing Advance Operation

You can check vacuum advance operation easily. Disconnect the vacuum line at the diaphragm housing and remove the distributor cap. Move the link by hand until the full-advanced position is reached. Place your finger over the vacuum port and release the link. It should barely move, if at all. After a few seconds, remove your finger from the vacuum port. The link should snap back to its original position without hesitation. The vacuum advance unit is serviced by replacement only.

Dirt, lack of lubrication, and distributor shaft/bearing wear affect the operation of the centrifugal advance. After a year's service, the mechanism should be inspected, cleaned, and properly lubricated. The weights and linkage must be completely clean and lightly lubricated with engine oil, even though GM maintains that no lubrication is required. Past experience has shown that the pivot pins have a tendency to wear when not lubricated. You may find nylon or Teflon-coated inserts in the advance weights of your distributor. This is GM's answer to the wear problem, but has not really solved it as of this writing. Lubricate the pivot pins lightly with engine oil.

Serving the HEI Distributor

A distributor tester is used to check distributor advance. This should be done by a professional shop with the necessary equipment and specs.

The Ignition System

Should you encounter an intermittent operation or "miss" with the HEI distributor, head directly to the pickup coil and disconnect its leads from the module. Ground one ohmmeter lead at the distributor housing and connect the other to one of the pickup coil leads. Calibrate the ohmmeter and read the X1000 scale—if the meter reads any less than infinity, the coil is at fault.

But suppose the meter reads infinity. Move the grounded ohmmeter lead to the other coil lead and calibrate the meter again. It should read between 500 and 1500 ohms. A reading on either side of this range also indicates a bad pickup coil. If the coil still checks out okay, the module is causing the problem.

Due to the compact engine compartment, a tachometer terminal extension lead is provided from the HEI distributor cap for easy test equipment connection.

The HEI distributor pivot pins tend to wear with centrifugal advance weight motion. Such wear throws the advance curve off and affects engine operation.

Distributor Replacement and Timing

If the distributor is removed from the engine for servicing, it should be replaced in exactly the same position, with the distributor housing and rotor in the same place relative to the engine as it was before removal. Before pulling the distributor, make a chalk mark on the top of the engine to indicate the position of the vacuum advance unit; then mark the rotor position directly on the distributor housing. If the engine was not rotated while the distributor was removed, replacing it in the same position will ensure that the engine will run. Once it is running, set the timing accurately with a timing light.

Since dwell is controlled by the electronic module inside the HEI distributor, initial ignition timing should not vary once it is correctly set—as long as the module is operating properly and there is no excessive distributor shaft or bearing wear. Despite the fact that timing normally should not vary, do not ignore a timing check during your tune-up. The amount of initial advance recommended for proper operation will be found on the emissions decal lo-

Proper spark plug cable routing is important. The cables should be arranged to prevent contact with each other, or with other accessory units.

An inexpensive plug cable tester will help locate defective cables.

cated in the engine compartment.

To time either the L4 or V6 engine, connect a timing light to the No. 1 spark plug wire and point the light at the timing marks on the crankshaft pulley and pointer. Loosen the distributor hold-down clamp and turn the entire housing with the engine idling while you check the position of the marks with the timing light. When the crankshaft mark aligns with the specified advance mark on the pointer, tighten the distributor hold-down in place. Turning the distributor housing opposite to the rotor's normal direction will advance the timing; turning it in the same direction as the rotor will retard it.

Spark Plugs

The spark plugs work under tremendous heat and pressure, firing as often as 10 times per second at high rpm. In the process, they are subjected to all sorts of corrosive contaminants from fuels and the combustion process, yet still last for thousands of miles. Your X-car, equipped with its HEI ignition, fires a high enough voltage to keep the plugs clean for as long as 30,000 miles under ideal circumstances.

Unfortunately, we don't drive under ideal circumstances, and it's hard to get the plugs to go the GM-recommended mileage without a thorough cleaning and regapping at the halfway point. It takes about twice as much voltage to fire a plug at high speeds as it does at idle, and three times the voltage under hard acceleration. If the engine cuts out under a heavy load, it's probably due to eroded plug gaps.

When replacing plugs, remove and install one plug wire and plug at a time. This prevents mixing

up the plug wires and lets you "read" each plug. Spark plugs should always be installed carefully and in clean surroundings. Tapered-seat plugs like the AC R43TSX must be installed according to the proper torque specs—about 15 ft.-lbs. If a torque wrench is not available, tighten the plugs finger tight and then an extra 1/16 turn. If you tighten them more, they may "seize" in place.

A seized or stuck plug can sometimes be loosened by tightening it a bit before trying to unscrew it, or by applying penetrating oil around the base of the plug in the well. After seized plugs are removed, check the cylinder head threads for dirt and damage. Clean them with a spark plug thread chaser, a tool available at most auto supply stores.

New plugs come pregapped, but should be checked before they are installed. Use a round wire gapping tool instead of a flat feeler gauge. The wire gauge should pass through the gap with a solid snap, but don't force it. If the gap must be adjusted, use the bending bar on the gap gauge to bend the side electrode. Never close the gap by banging the plug against a hard surface—this can crack the porcelain insulation. And don't use a screwdriver to open the gap—you can damage the electrode.

If the plugs are removed at 10,000 to 15,000 miles, they can be restored to almost like-new condition by a sandblast cleaning. You can have this done at any garage with a plug cleaner—those sold in auto supply stores will not do a satisfactory job. Sandblast cleaning increases rather than decreases a plug's voltage requirement. It not only removes the conductive deposits from the electrodes, but the abrasive cleaning action tends to round them off. You should always file spark plug electrodes to a sharp, square shape after cleaning. This will restore the plug to close to its original voltage requirement.

After cleaning and filing, always regap used plugs to their original specification. A gap that's too close makes a rough idle, and one that's too wide increases the amount of voltage required to fire it, causing a miss during high-speed acceleration.

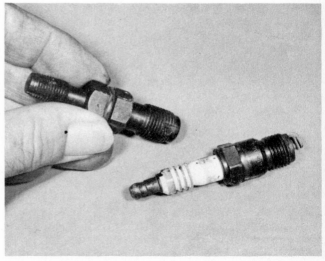

A spark plug thread chaser is used to clean dirty or seized plug hole threads before installing new plugs.

The Ignition System

Secondary Wiring

HEI spark plug wires are not really wire at all, but a carbon-impregnated core conductor surrounded by a soft silicone rubber jacket. Silicone has two major virtues: it withstands the high engine compartment temperatures better than other materials, and it is an excellent insulator for the higher HEI voltage. It also has one very big fault: it's very soft and can be easily damaged by test equipment leads or rough handling.

Since the silicone spark plug connectors form a very tight seal on the plug, always rotate the connector back and forth before trying to remove it from the plug terminal. Be sure to pull on the connector, not the wire, or you may cause an internal break in the conductor. There are several good plug wire pliers available which will give you a good grasp on the connector without risking the possibility of burning yourself on a hot block or manifold.

When using test equipment, never prick a hole in the plug wire insulation jacket to make a connection. Such small punctures do not seal, but allow electricity to jump to a ground where the wire passes by the engine. Avoid trying to force a probe or test equipment lead between the connector and the wire.

Plug wires are subjected to repeated extremes in temperature, moisture, oil and grease exposure, engine vibration, and terminal corrosion, among other problems. These factors tend to cause plug wires to age rapidly. Whenever you're working under the hood, check the wires visually for any signs of deterioration. If the connector or wire jacket is excessively spongy, brittle, or burned, the wire should be replaced.

When servicing the spark plugs, remove and examine one wire at a time. Wipe it with a kerosene-moistened cloth to remove any grease or oil, and then wipe it dry with a clean cloth. Gently bend the wire along its entire length. Any signs of chafing or cracked or brittle insulation, and the wire should be replaced.

When installing a new wire set, remove and install one wire at a time. Take pains to route each new wire exactly as the old one was routed. Make sure that they are secured in the wire retainer or that looms are used to keep them separate and away from hot surfaces. Poor plug wire routing will lead to crossfiring plugs or shorting to ground and a misfire.

The HEI distributor looks imposing in or out of the engine, but this should not prevent you from servicing it properly. To help you along, we've included a complete disassembly/reassembly sequence on the following pages. One precaution—if the shaft bushing appears to be worn excessively, don't try to remove it from the housing. The shaft bushing and distributor housing are replaced as a complete unit, not individually.

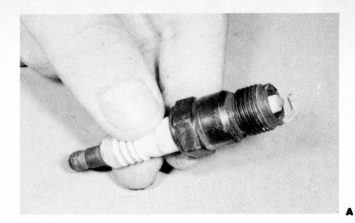

A

B

C

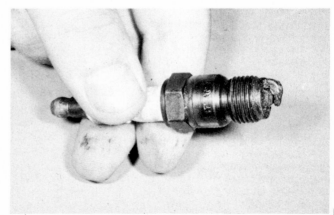

D

Spark plug condition can tell much about an engine's health. The plug in (A) shows normal wear, while the electrode in (B) is covered with scavenger deposits (excessive low-speed driving). Preignition caused the electrode damage shown in (C), and the oil-fouled plug in (D) indicates worn rings or valve guides.

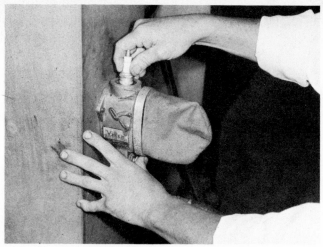

An abrasive-type spark plug cleaner is the only way to renovate used plugs. Be sure to blow debris from the plug tip with compressed air after cleaning.

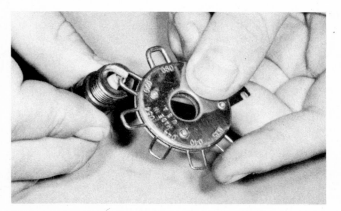

Always check the plug gap with a round wire feeler gauge.

After cleaning, sharpen plug electrodes with an ignition point file. If electrodes are badly rounded, plugs should be replaced with new ones.

L4 Distributor Hold-Down

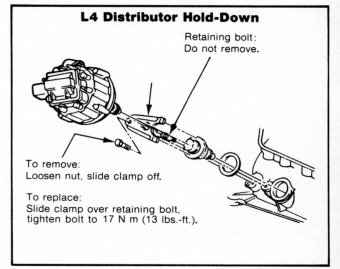

Retaining bolt:
Do not remove.

To remove:
Loosen nut, slide clamp off.

To replace:
Slide clamp over retaining bolt,
tighten bolt to 17 N m (13 lbs.-ft.).

L4 Spark Plug Wire Routing

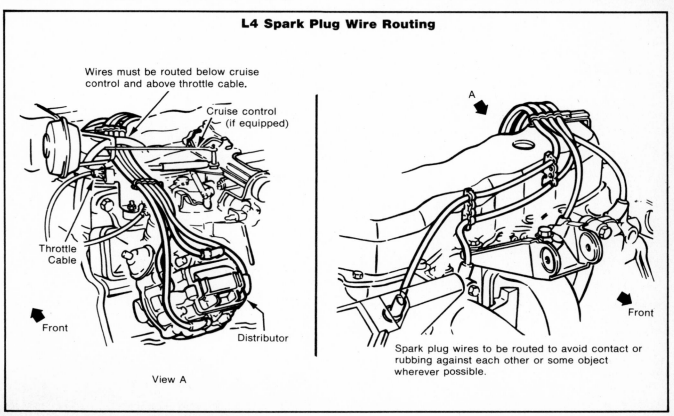

Wires must be routed below cruise
control and above throttle cable.

Cruise control
(if equipped)

Throttle
Cable

Front

Distributor

View A

A

Front

Spark plug wires to be routed to avoid contact or
rubbing against each other or some object
wherever possible.

The Ignition System-HEI L4 Distributor Overhaul

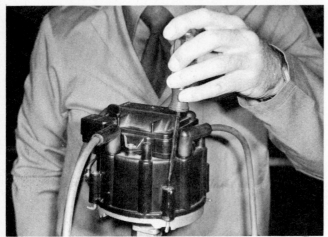

1. The L4 and V6 distributor stripdown are the same procedure. Four turn latches hold cap to housing. Latches will turn 90 degrees in one direction only.

2. Unclip distributor module connector lead from the distributor cap housing by carefully prying it free with a screwdriver blade—do not try to pull it out by hand.

3. Remove the plug wires from the cap; then place the cap on a flat surface and remove the coil cover. Four cap screws hold the cap and coil together. Remove them and lift out the coil.

4. Use a small screwdriver to push the tach and battery lead clips from the cap connector. The ground lead does not have to be removed in order to replace the coil.

5. An enclosed coil creates heat and moisture, so a large rubber seal is used to absorb moisture and prevent shorting. Replace the seal if it has lost flexibility.

6. With the seal removed, the carbon button and spring can be lifted out. Don't install the button without the spring or you'll have an opening between the button and coil secondary contact.

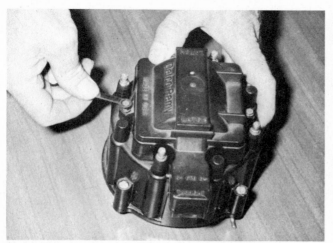

7. Replace the coil in the cap, install the leads in the connector, and replace the cap screws to secure the coil. Install the cover over the coil and tighten the two attaching screws.

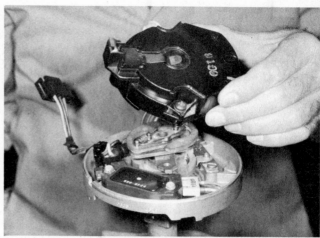

8. The rotor is attached to the centrifugal advance mechanism by two screws. Loosen the screws, remove the rotor, and inspect for hairline cracks, burned contacts, etc.

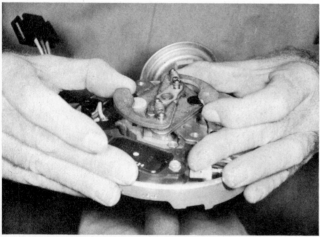

9. To check the centrifugal advance mechanism for wear, pull both advance weights out as far as they will go and release, watching the action as they swing back into place.

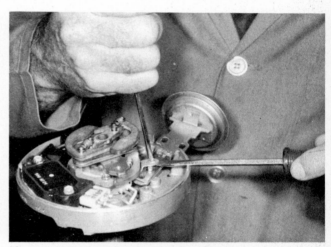

10. To remove the vacuum advance diaphragm, press down with a pair of screwdrivers as shown to unlock the linkage foot from the pole piece attaching the link.

11. Remove the screw holding the capacitor in place. The capacitor, bracket, and module connector harness can be lifted out as a single unit and replaced the same way.

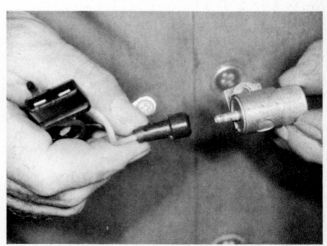

12. Disconnect the capacitor from the module connector harness by pulling them apart. Slip the old capacitor from the bracket, center the new one, and plug it back into the harness.

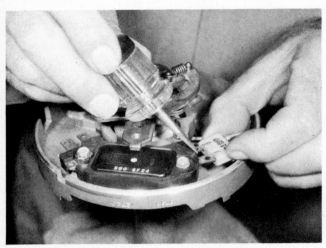

13. To remove the module, use a screwdriver blade to pry the connector lead from the module prongs—do not attempt to remove by wiggling or pulling the connector free by hand.

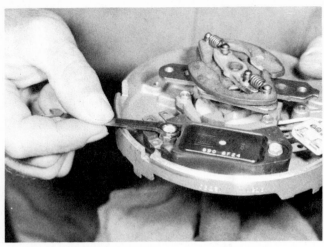

14. With the module disconnected, loosen the attaching screws. Several different modules are now used—be sure to replace it with one bearing the same part number.

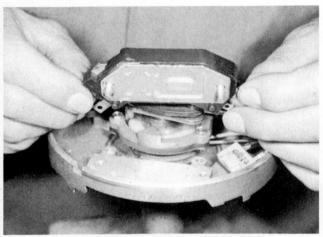

15. You should find silicone grease on the underside of the module, as well as on the housing where it fits. This is necessary for proper module operation.

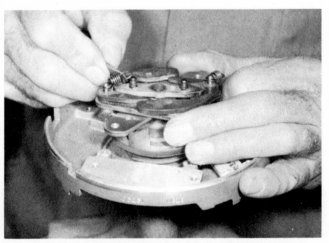

16. Unclip the centrifugal advance weight attaching springs. Remove the weights and inspect the pivot pins for wear; then check the Teflon inserts in the weights for wear or damage.

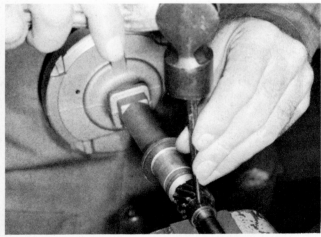

17. Support the distributor shaft and tap out the drive gear retaining roll pin. This housing is fitted with two brass bushings. Do not damage them or the housing will have to be replaced.

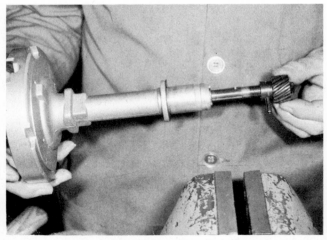

18. The drive gear, shim, and tanged washer will now slip off the shaft end. Clean the shaft with crocus cloth to remove any burrs and note the dimple in the drive gear.

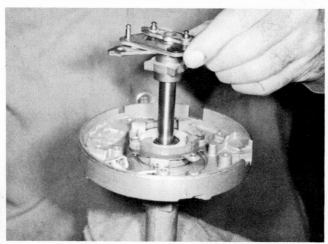

19. Remove the shaft with the advance mechanism by pulling it straight up and out of the housing as shown. If the shaft is burred, it will damage the housing bushings during removal/installation.

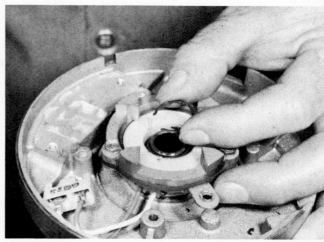

20. This tiny wave washer must be pried carefully from its slot at the top of the distributor shaft before the stationary tooth assembly can be removed—an ingenious way of holding things together.

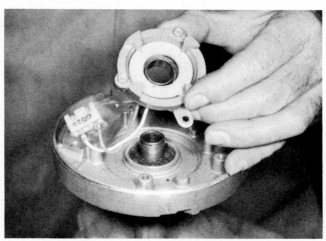

21. Loosen the cap screws holding stationary tooth assembly in housing. If the pickup coil tests out with more than 800 ohms resistance, expect problems.

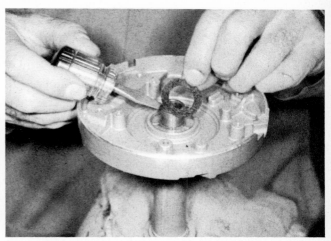

22. You'll find this felt washer under the stationary tooth assembly. It rests on top of a lubricant reservoir covered with a plastic shield. Lubricate the washer.

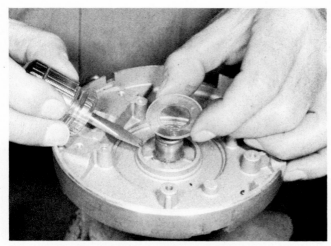

23. To check the lubricant under the plastic shield, remove the shield with a screwdriver blade. Be sure to replace the shield and washer before beginning reassembly.

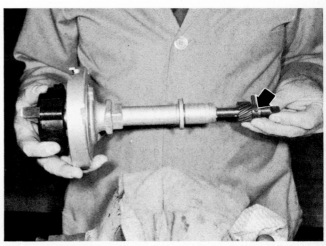

24. Remember the drive gear dimple (arrow)? It must be aligned with the rotor contact when replacing the drive gear. Support the shaft, install the roll pin, and reassemble the distributor.

6

The Fuel System

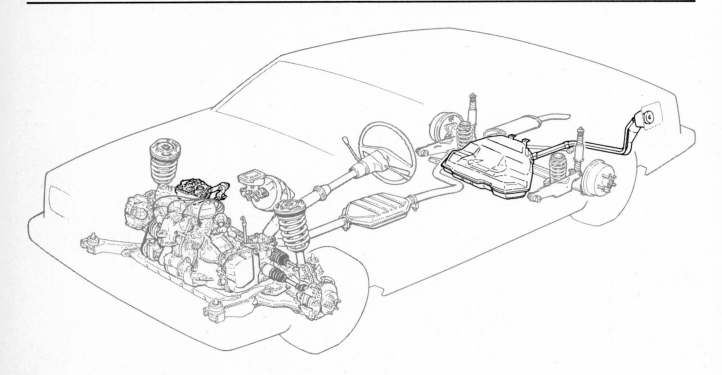

Transporting gasoline from the fuel tank to the engine has become quite complicated in recent years. All X-cars use an evaporative emissions control system, which includes the fuel tank and lines connecting it to the carburetor and a charcoal vapor canister in the engine compartment. The system is designed to prevent the escape of raw fuel vapors created by fuel expansion in the tank or in the carburetor float bowl. Instead of allowing such vapors to escape, the system stores them for combustion when the engine is running.

The fuel tank has a fill-limiting feature created by the use of a special filler neck and vent lines. This keeps at least 10 percent of the tank's volume open for expansion, even when the tank is "full" of gasoline. An emissions line carries fuel vapors from the tank forward to the carbon canister. Connected to the carburetor, this canister stores the vapors until they can be burned by the engine. The canister

contains a filter pad which should be replaced every 30,000 miles, but if the carbon, or charcoal, element becomes water-saturated (it draws water vapors from the fuel vapors), the canister must be replaced with a new one.

Except for the carburetor, fuel system components are designed to be replaced as units. Fuel and vapor return lines are not sold as units, however, but must be made up from bulk rolls of steel tubing, the necessary neoprene hoses, and clamps. The main fuel line is connected to an in-tank fuel filter located at the pickup end. While it normally won't require any service, it can be replaced. To do so, the fuel tank must first be removed from the car. The sending unit is then removed from the tank.

The vapor and main feed lines run under the body floor pan and are held in place by clips. These lines are welded steel tubing, except for the neoprene connections used where line movement or flexing takes place. If it's necessary to replace such connections, use only fuel-impervious hoses and clamp them securely to the steel tubing at each end.

Although located underneath the car, the fuel lines are quite well protected from stones and other objects that might be thrown up by the wheels. Just the same, it's a good idea to check all the fuel and emissions lines throughout their entire lengths to see if any part of the steel lines has been pinched or dented, and to make sure that the flexible hoses do not show signs of deterioration.

Flexible hose material may gradually slough off the inner walls and partially, or even fully, clog the system in time. If blockage of one or more lines seems to be the problem, disconnect the suspected line at each end and then blow it out with compressed air.

The main fuel line leads to the fuel pump, a mechanically actuated device which is driven by the engine camshaft to pump fuel from the tank and up to the induction system. Fuel pumps incorporate a diaphragm which is mechanically stroked by actuating linkage.

If your L4 engine cuts out on turns, remove the vent/screen.

Fuel Pump Performance

The fuel pumps used on both the 4 and 6-cylinder X-car engines are integral, nonserviceable units and are replaced when they malfunction instead of being rebuilt.

The fuel pump should not be suspected of failure *unless* it fails to meet specifications for pressure and flow. A cracked or broken diaphragm will allow fuel to leak out onto the ground and thus can't pump enough fuel to meet the engine's requirements. The pressure can be checked by disconnecting the fuel line from the carburetor and connecting a pressure gauge. When testing a fuel pump with a gauge, you'll find a line clamp helpful. Use a T-fitting to allow fuel to be pumped past the gauge when the clamp pressure is relieved. Make your test by cranking the engine to get fuel pressure with the clamp relieved (bypassing the gauge); then shut off the clamp and take your gauge reading. The 4-cylinder fuel pump should deliver 6.5-8 psi, while the V6 pump is rated at 6-7.5 psi. Both pumps should be capable of flowing a pint of fuel every 30 seconds at cranking speed.

Fuel Pump Removal and Replacement

As with most other cars, the fuel pump is located in the most inaccessible part of the engine compartment, and although locating it may not be difficult, removal/replacement is something of a chore. This is particularly true of the 4-cylinder pump, which is located on the rear of the engine to the left of the oil filter and under the intake manifold. The V6 pump is more convenient to service. It's located on the front of the engine (also next to the oil filter) and is protected by a metal shield.

Regardless of which engine you have, the procedure is essentially the same. You simply disconnect and plug the lines attached to the pump. Then remove the two hex-head bolts holding the pump to

the engine block and remove the pump.

When you loosen or reconnect a line, always use two wrenches—one to hold the inner fitting and the other to turn the outer fitting. Compare the pump removed from the engine to the replacement pump. There may be some fittings on the old pump which will have to be transferred to the new one. If such fittings are directional, be sure to install them on the new pump facing in the same direction as on the old unit.

To install a new fuel pump, remove all old gasket material on the pump mounting pad at the engine block. Apply oil-resistant sealer to both sides of a new gasket and position it on the pump flange. Install the pump against the mounting pad and make certain that the rocker arm rides on the camshaft's eccentric. The V6 pump uses a spring-loaded pushrod instead of a rocker arm. Press the pump tightly against the pad, install the hex-head bolts, and alternately tighten them snugly. Reconnect the lines, using new clamps; then start the engine and let it idle while you check for leaks.

The Carburetor

All X-cars use a 2-barrel, model 2SE Rochester Varajet carburetor (or E2SE in California). Carburetors used on the 4-cylinder engine differ slightly from those fitted to the V6 and are thus not interchangeable. For example, a single-vacuum choke break is on the L4 engine, while a dual-vacuum break is found on V6 carburetors.

The E2SE differs from the 2SE in that it incorporates an electrically operated mixture control solenoid in the air horn. Pulsed by signals from the C-4 electronic control module (see Chapter 7), this solenoid adjusts the air/fuel ratio to keep it as near as possible to the ideal ratio. Both carburetor models have factory-sealed idle-mixture needles and a nonadjustable (tamperproof) choke cover designed to discourage do-it-yourself adjustments.

Most problems attributed to the carburetor are really caused by ignition timing, spark plugs, loss of compression, inadequate fuel delivery to the carburetor, vacuum leaks, or even a clogged air cleaner filter. The carburetor itself seldom gives much trouble during normal operation. It has so few moving parts that there really isn't much in it to wear out. The throttle shaft and accelerator pump are prob-

The Fuel System

ably the biggest offenders.

The throttle shaft wears at its bushings from the pressure of the throttle return spring. This may let in too much or too little air to the engine. When the accelerator pump plunger wears out and doesn't squirt as much as it should, the result is a flat spot (hesitation) when the driver steps on the gas.

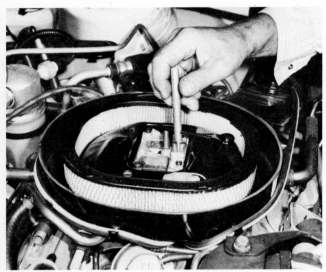

A special screwdriver is then used to reach jet at bottom of well under screen. Lightly bottom screw and back out about 2½ turns adjusting carburetor.

Overhauling the Carburetor

Once the passages and jets begin to clog up with gum, varnish, or dirt, the carburetor will require an overhaul if it is to work properly. Rebuilding a carburetor isn't as difficult as it looks, provided you approach the job in an orderly manner. It's quite possible for a beginner to remove, rebuild, and replace his own carburetor with no difficulty, as long as he works carefully, follows a logical sequence, uses common sense, and has patience.

If you decide to rebuild the carburetor yourself, make sure to buy the overhaul kit from your GM dealer *before* you touch the carburetor. To get the correct kit, you'll need the numbers and letters stamped on the carburetor. This model identification information will be found on the carburetor near the choke housing.

Once you have the correct overhaul kit, you can remove the carburetor from the engine and disassemble it. Place the nonreplaceable parts (the ones you'll reuse) in a small container to prevent them from becoming lost, and dispose of all neoprene O-rings and gaskets that will be replaced upon reassembly. Carburetor work is a matter of good judgment. If you only plan to replace a leaking air horn gasket, it's more practical to leave the carburetor on the engine.

If the carburetor is taken apart for a complete cleaning, all solenoids, sensors, diaphragms, plas-

tic and rubber parts should be removed before the body is immersed in the cleaning solvent. You can leave the jets in place, and don't try to remove any screws or other parts that are staked in place. Staked parts are preset at the factory and their adjustment should not be attempted in the field, especially by an amateur.

Use a fresh, powerful immersion-type carburetor cleaner. If you don't have a small mesh basket handy for lowering the small parts into the solution container, punch a few small holes in the bottom of a small coffee can. Use this to hold the small parts and hook a metal clothes hanger around the main body, throttle body, and air horn. (Never put your hands in it, and don't let it splash in your eyes.)

Depending upon how fresh the solvent is, and how dirty the carburetor, cleaning will take anywhere from half an hour to several hours. When the parts look bright and clean as you lift them from the solution, the job is finished. Drain the parts and reimmerse them into a second solution of fresh solvent for a few minutes. When you remove them a second time, let the parts drain and then blow them dry with compressed air.

The most important, and generally the only, adjustment needed inside the carburetor is the float level. Surging, dying, hesitation, rich or lean running—all these conditions can be caused by an incorrect float level. Some engines may even die on turns if the float level isn't set correctly. The overhaul kit instructions will show how to make the necessary adjustments.

Above all, work carefully to avoid bending or otherwise damaging any parts. Don't force anything in place—if it doesn't go easily, you're doing something wrong or in the wrong sequence.

Fuel pump location on the V6 (A) is under a heat shield beside the oil filter. On the L4 (B), it's also beside the oil filter, but on the back of the engine.

Carburetor Specifications

Carb No.	Float Adjustment (ins.)	Pump Adjustment (ins.)	Fast Idle Adjustment (bench) (No. turns after (cam contact)	A/C Idle Speed RPM		Non-A/C Idle Speed RPM	
				Sol.	Curb.	Curb.	Basic
17059614	3/16	1/2	3	—	—	650D	500D
17059615	3/16	5/32	3	—	—	1000N	500N
17059616	3/16	1/2	3	650D	900D	—	—
17059617	3/16	5/32	3	1000N	1300N	—	—
17059650	3/16	3/32	3	—	—	700D	NA
17059651	3/16	3/32	3	—	—	750N	1200N
17059652	3/16	3/32	3	700D	850D	—	—
17059653	3/16	3/32	3	750N	1200N	—	—
17059714	11/16	5/32	3	—	—	650D	500D
17059715	11/16	3/32	3	—	—	1000N	500N
17059716	11/16	5/32	3	650D	850D	—	—
17059717	11/16	3/32	3	1000N	1200N	—	—
17059760	1/8	5/64	3	—	—	700D	NA
17059762	1/8	5/64	3	700D	800D	—	—
17059763	1/8	5/64	3	750N	NA	—	—
17059618	3/16	1/2	3	—	—	650D	500D
17059619	3/16	5/32	3	—	—	1000N	500N
17059620	3/16	1/2	3	650D	900D	—	—
17059621	3/16	5/32	3	1000N	1300N	—	—

Carb No.	Choke Coil Lever (ins.)	Choke Rod (deg.)	Air Valve Rod (ins.)	Vacuum Break (deg.)		Unloader (deg.)	Secondary Lockout (ins.)	Fast Idle RPM
				Pri.	Sec.			
17059614	.085	18	—	17	—	36	—	2600
17059615	.085	18	—	19	—	36	—	2600
17059616	.085	18	—	17	—	36	—	2600
17059617	.085	18	—	19	—	36	—	2600
17059650	.085	27	.025	30	38	30	—	2000
17059651	.085	27	.025	22	23	30	—	1900
17059652	.085	27	.025	30	38	30	—	2000
17059653	.085	27	.025	22	23	30	—	1900
17059714	.085	18	—	23	—	32	—	2600
17059715	.085	18	—	25	—	32	—	2200
17059716	.085	18	—	23	—	32	—	2600
17059717	.085	18	—	25	—	32	—	2200
17059760	.085	17.5	.025	20	33	35	—	2000
17059762	.085	17.5	.025	20	33	35	.120	2000
17059763	.085	17.5	.025	20	33	35	.120	2000
17059618	.085	18	—	17	—	36	.120	2600
17059619	.085	18	—	19	—	36	—	2600
17059620	.085	18	—	17	—	36	—	2600
17059621	.085	18	—	19	—	36	—	2600

CAUTION

While all versions of the Rochester 2SE and E2SE carburetors are essentially the same, there are a number of individual variations according to model year and engine/transmission application. Since GM constantly revises the calibration of the carburetors used from one model year to another, the procedures which follow are to be regarded as being representative of the overhaul procedures to be followed. However, not all carburetors will contain the same components in the same sequence, operate exactly the same, or even be adjusted alike. To prevent improper functioning when overhauling your carburetor, do not hesitate to check with your local GM dealership should you encounter differences from those shown in our pictorial how-to sequences.

1. A Rochester E2SE is used on X-cars equipped with the C-4 emission system. Begin the overhaul by unbolting the solenoid bracket at two points on the carburetor air horn.

2. With the bracket disconnected, the solenoid and vacuum break diaphragm linkage can be disengaged and assembly removed from the carburetor. Cleaning solvent will damage both units.

3. Some carburetors use a pump rod clip. This must be removed to disengage the pump rod from the hole in the pump lever. If no clip is used, remove the pump lever screw to disengage the pump rod.

4. To unhook the remaining linkage, unbolt the fast-idle cam and remove it. This is easier than trying to disengage the linkage when the air horn is removed.

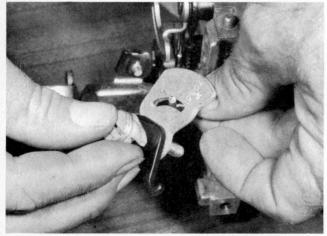

5. With the fast-idle cam removed, rotate it to unhook the fast-idle cam rod from the slot in the cam and place the assembly to one side. New float bowls come with the fast-idle cam attached.

6. Remove the three screws holding the mixture control solenoid in the air horn. Lift the solenoid with a twisting motion. Remove and discard the seal and retainer on the plunger end.

7. Remove the air horn attaching screws and lock washers. The L4 version uses six screws; V6 carburetor has seven. Tap the air horn gently with a rubber mallet to break the seal.

8. Separate the air horn from the float bowl and rotate it to disengage the rest of the linkage. Set the air horn upside down on your workbench and then move the float bowl out of the way.

9. Push the throttle position sensor plunger through the seal in the air horn and remove it; then use small screwdriver to pry out seal and retainer. Discard both as new ones are used for reassembly.

10. If the accelerator pump plunger remains in the air horn, remove it and pry out the pump seal and retainer. These are also discarded, as new ones will be installed during reassembly.

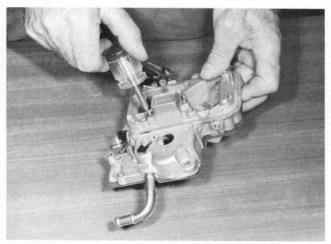

11. Remove the two attaching screws and lift the vent/screen assembly from the air horn. Further disassembly of the air horn is not required for cleaning purposes.

12. The accelerator pump return spring is located in the pump bore of float bowl. Remove the spring and place it with the pump plunger. Install the new piston on the plunger.

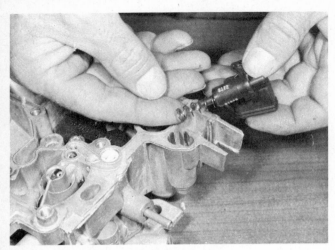

13. To remove the throttle position sensor, push up from the bottom on the electrical connector. The spring in the bottom of the TPS well in the bowl should also be removed.

14. Catch the edge of the plastic filler block over the float valve with a fingertip and lift up enough to remove it from the carburetor. (Don't forget to reinstall this!)

15. Pull up on the retaining pin to remove the float assembly and valve. The float valve may drop off and remain in the seat, so take a good look at the assembly before removing it.

16. If the valve remains in the seat, remove it with the clip attached. The overhaul kit will contain a new float valve, which should be installed during reassembly.

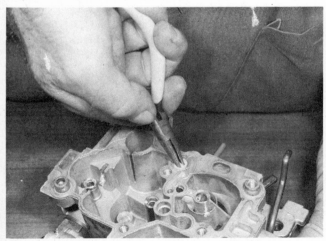

17. Use a small slide hammer or needle-nose pliers to remove the plastic retainer holding the pump discharge spring/check ball. Do not pry it out, as this can damage the bowl casting.

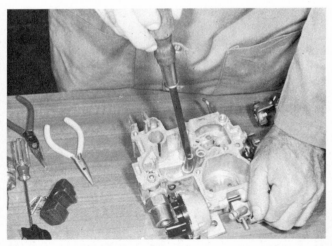

18. Use a wide-blade screwdriver to remove the extended metering jet from the float bowl. Do not change the adjustment of the calibration screw inside the jet—this is factory-set.

19. Use a wide-blade screwdriver to remove the float valve seat and gasket. The new seat and gasket should be installed during reassembly. Be sure to tighten snugly.

20. Turn the float bowl over and remove the fuel inlet/filter/spring assembly if it was not removed when the carburetor was taken off the car. Install a new filter during reassembly with the hole facing the nut.

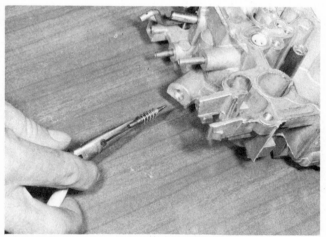

21. The idle mixture needle is covered with a staked plug (not shown). Do not remove the plug or needle unless it is necessary to replace the needle.

22. Turn the float bowl over and remove the four screws holding the throttle body to the float bowl. Don't immerse the float bowl completely in cleaner as the choke housing is a sealed unit.

23. Blow out the passages with compressed air and install the metering jet, pump discharge assembly, plastic retainer, float valve seat, and float assembly.

24. To check the float action, hold the valve in the seat and press down on the retaining pin. The float measurement is taken from on top of the float to the casting edge. Adjustment instructions are in the kit.

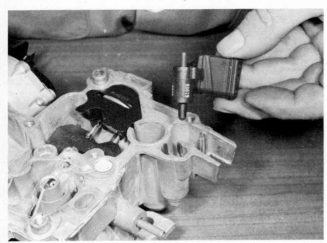

25. *Press the plastic block over the float, drop the TPS spring in the well slot, and press the throttle position solenoid in place. Replace the TPS plunger with a new seal in the air horn. Stake the seal in place.*

26. *Install the accelerator pump and spring in the pump well; then fit the new gasket in position on the float bowl and replace the air horn, connecting the linkage properly.*

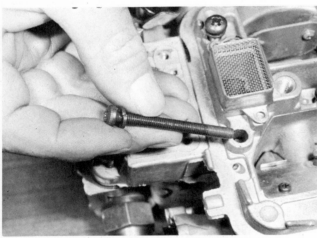

27. *Replace the vent/screen assembly and install the attaching bolts with lock washers. Tighten the bolts evenly and alternately to draw the air horn down without warping it.*

28. *Place the new mixture control solenoid gasket on the air horn. Lightly coat the rubber seal on the end of the solenoid stem with light engine oil to make installation easier.*

29. *Install the mixture control solenoid on the air horn by aligning the stem with the recess in the bottom of the bowl. Twist the solenoid while pressing down to guide the stem seal in place.*

30. *Attach the vacuum diaphragm to the float bowl and reconnect the intermediate choke rod using the new retaining clip. The plastic bushing under the clip is reused, not replaced.*

31. Reconnect the choke linkage (A), fit the pump arm over the rod, and install the clip. With the non-clip model, attach the arm to the rod and replace the screw (B).

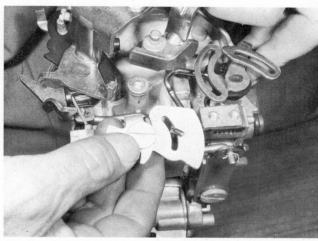

32. Connect the fast-idle cam rod to the choke link, fit the end of the rod in the fast-idle cam, and rotate the cam to the proper position; then install the attaching screw finger-tight.

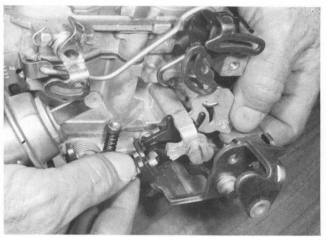

33. Check the cam/rod installation—it should look exactly like this before the cam attaching screw is tightened in place. The L4's carburetor linkage is less complicated.

34. Connect the secondary vacuum break diaphragm to the choke valve and press the other end into the plastic bushing on the diaphragm link. Install the new retaining clip.

35. Position the solenoid to connect the air valve rod; then swivel the solenoid assembly into the proper position and check the rod operation for binding.

36. Install the two screws holding the solenoid bracket to the float bowl and air horn. Reconnect the primary-side vacuum diaphragm vacuum line to the carburetor.

1. To service the carburetor, the air cleaner housing must be removed. Disconnect the ducting, remove the cover nuts, and unhook the vacuum lines and hoses.

2. The carburetor is attached to the EGR spacer atop the manifold—don't confuse attaching nuts. Use a socket and extension to loosen nuts at front and rear of carburetor base.

3. Since finger space is very limited around the carburetor, a pocket magnet will come in handy if the nut slips off the manifold stud and falls into a tight space.

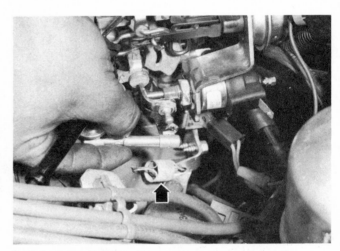

4. Unhook the throttle return spring (arrow) and pull the throttle lever clip from the linkage stud. In some cases, you may need to pry the lever/stud apart with a screwdriver.

5. Disconnect the carburetor mixture control solenoid, if your carburetor is so equipped. Tuck the electrical connector under the air conditioning hoses, out of the way.

6. To unhook the vapor return line, squeeze the clamp nearest the carburetor with pliers and pry it to the rear of the line with a screwdriver; then pull the hose from the carburetor fitting.

7. Unscrew the fuel inlet nut and pull the fuel line from the carburetor inlet. Plug the end of the fuel line to prevent gasoline and fumes from leaking out.

8. Check the carburetor thoroughly, and disconnect any remaining electrical lines; then pry the vacuum lines from the nipples at the rear of the carburetor.

9. The carburetor should now be ready to remove from the manifold. Grasp it by the air cleaner attaching studs and lift the assembly straight up and off.

10. Place the carburetor on a flat surface. It's a good idea to set it on a clean cloth to prevent any accidental damage to the throttle plates or mounting flange.

11. Inspect the carburetor gasket on the manifold for damage or leaking. Now is a good time to check the operation of the EGR valve with the carburetor out of the way.

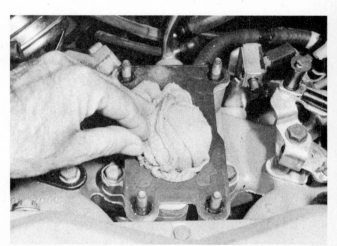

12. Stuff a clean cloth into the manifold throats to prevent any contamination or small parts from falling in. Carburetor replacement is the reverse of removal.

7

Emissions Controls

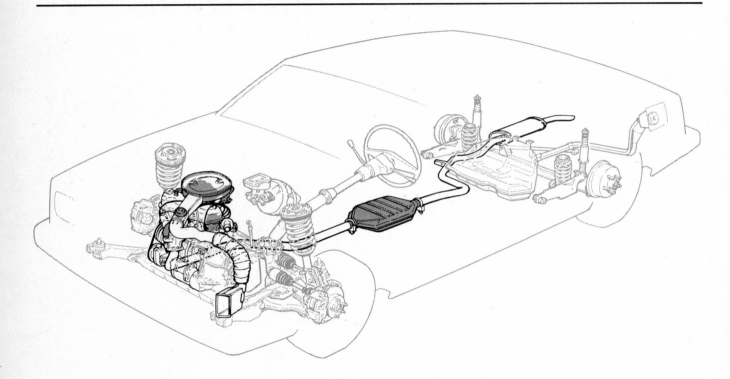

All X-car engines are fitted with various systems designed to reduce the amount of pollutants passed into the atmosphere. The complexity of the emissions control devices on your particular X-car depends upon the model year and where it was sold. Servicing the C-4 system when it fails is best left to your GM dealer, who has the trained personnel and specialized test equipment to diagnose and correct the problem. But there are some emissions systems fitted to all X-cars that you can and should monitor/maintain yourself.

Inlet Air Temp Regulation

The air cleaner and its connecting hoses and vacuum lines make up this emissions control system. It maintains the temperature of the air entering the carburetor at approximately 77-123 degrees F. whenever the required heated or cool air

is available. Air temperature held at a constant and moderately high temperature improves engine warm-up, minimizes carburetor icing, and allows the use of a leaner carburetor air/fuel mixture.

Air for the carburetor intake is introduced directly from the exhaust manifold through a baffle or shroud, called a heat stove, and a tube connecting it to the air cleaner snorkel. A diaphragm-type vacuum motor and spring operate a heat control door in the snorkel to let in cooler air from outside the vehicle, while shutting off the hot air from the heat stove.

A bimetal temperature sensor located inside the air cleaner housing controls the vacuum motor. On a cold engine that's not running, the diaphragm spring holds the door wide open. But once the engine has been started and manifold vacuum builds up to about 7 inches or more, the vacuum motor will override the spring, closing the heat control door

With all the vacuum-operated emissions devices on the L4 and V6 engines, a hand vacuum pump is very useful in checking vacuum break operation.

and shutting off the air intake from the fresh air duct. Some X-car engines have a sensor check valve installed. This delays the heat control door opening when intake air is cold and the vacuum signal is reduced. The duration of delay varies according to the surrounding temperature.

Normally, the bimetal temperature sensor acts as a modulator to mix the hot and cold air properly by controlling the position of the door. When the air cleaner temperature rises above the system design temperature, the sensor opens a valve to bleed additional air into the vacuum line. If it falls below the design temperature, the air bleed is closed to let more manifold vacuum reach the vacuum motor. The result of this operation is to close off outside air during conditions of high vacuum, such as idle, cruise, or deceleration, and to introduce outside air for maximum airflow during periods of low vacuum or acceleration.

When the system fails, the heat control door will generally remain open, allowing only air from the fresh air duct to enter. This shouldn't bother engine operation during warm weather, but when the temperature dips, you'll notice hesitation, surging, sagging, or stalling. These symptoms mean that a quick check of the air cleaner's operation is in order before you blame the carburetor for being set too lean.

What can go wrong? Well, let's troubleshoot the air cleaner for a few minutes, since improper functioning of the system will affect both the emissions level and how your engine runs. If you suspect an air cleaner malfunction, look first to make sure that all vacuum lines are in good order and are correctly connected. A pinched or cracked line may often be the problem. Next, remove the air cleaner from the carburetor and disconnect the vacuum diaphragm hose either at the sensor or at the vacuum motor. Use a hand-operated vacuum pump to apply about 10 inches of vacuum to the diaphragm. If a hand pump is not available, you can apply your mouth to the vacuum line and suck in. The vacuum applied

should cause the heat control door to close completely. To make certain that there are no vacuum leaks, pinch or clamp the hose to trap the vacuum in the line. If the door moves from its closed position, you've got a vacuum leak in the diaphragm and the vacuum motor must be replaced.

You can also remove and test the sensor unit like a thermostat by immersing it in hot water. This will tell you if it's unseating the bleed valve properly, but a more convenient way to check if it's working correctly is to reconnect the air cleaner on the carburetor and start the engine. The heat control door should immediately close, but as the engine warms up, it will begin to open gradually, letting a mixture of heated and cooler outside air enter. This will tell you if the sensor is actually working, but it won't tell you if the temperature range of operation is correct. Of course, you shouldn't rule out the possibility of binding linkage in the heat control door operation.

Experience would suggest that you're most likely to encounter problems with the air cleaner if you drop it on the floor, fail to keep the air intake and heat control door free of dirt and grease buildup, accidentally pinch the vacuum lines when you replace the unit on the carburetor, or run it with a dirty filter element.

Dropping the air cleaner housing can easily damage the vacuum motor, temperature sensor, or the connecting linkage between the diaphragm and heat control door. Dirt and grease accumulation can prevent proper door movement, while pinching the vacuum lines can cause a leak or restrict the

A vacuum gauge is used to check the EGR valve operation.

Emissions Controls

amount of vacuum applied. And a really dirty air filter element will not only affect temperature sensor operation, but it will also distort the air/fuel mixture. This unit is located inside the filter circumference, and air must pass through it to reach the sensor.

Incidentally, you'll now find a separate small crankcase ventilation filter pack installed inside some X-car air cleaners. This filter acts to trap oil and other contaminants when blow-by gases reverse their direction under heavy engine load and travel back through the PCV valve inlet hose into the air cleaner. This filter should be replaced at the same time the air filter element is replaced. If the filter becomes excessively dirty, it will reduce the effectiveness of the PCV system, which we'll examine shortly.

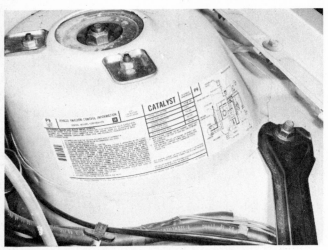

The Vehicle Emission Control Information decal contains specific adjustment procedures and specs for the car to which it is attached, and supersedes any other published data.

One final aspect of air cleaner maintenance concerns the fresh-air ducting. The 4-cylinder engine uses a rigid plastic tube connected between the air cleaner snorkel and the fresh-air inlet duct which draws air in from outside the engine compartment. There are several advantages to using an enclosed ducting system. It prefilters air entering the system and prevents the accumulation of engine compartment debris and contaminants which can affect operation of the heat control door. But the rigid plastic tubes tend to crack easily from engine vibration, especially at the sharp bend where they connect to the air cleaner snorkel. Since cracking of the tube will adversely affect heat control door operation, keep a close eye on it and replace any cracked tube as soon as possible.

Positive Crankcase Ventilation

This is the familiar PCV system, and all X-car engines use it. A sealed oil-filler cap prevents crankcase gases from escaping under no-vacuum conditions. A tube from the air cleaner goes to

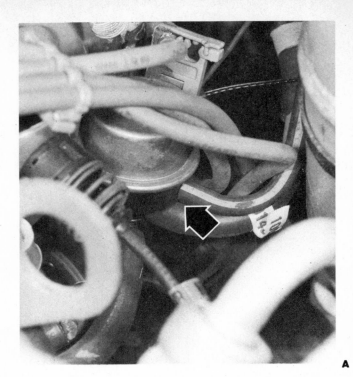

A

B

The decel valve is located in different positions on the L4 (A) and V6 (B) engines.

the rocker cover, carrying fresh air through the air cleaner filter and down into the crankcase. From that point, the fresh air mixes with blow-by gases created during combustion and passes through a hose to the intake manifold. This hose contains a metering or PCV valve operated by engine vacuum to control the amount of crankcase vapors which enter the intake system at any given time.

During times when the PCV system is under zero-vacuum conditions, there is no suction on the crankcase, but the gases go from the rocker cover through the hose into the air cleaner, where they are drawn into the intake manifold through the car-

Periodic inspection of all vacuum hoses and lines will reveal those that need replacement.

Exhaust Gas Recirculation

The EGR system reduces the formation of NOX by metering hot exhaust gases into the intake manifold. These gases dilute the air/fuel mixture and thus reduce the peak flame temperature during combustion. EGR systems are designed to operate only above a certain engine speed, usually 2500-3000 rpm, as the diluted mixture will cause a rough engine idle.

Those hot exhaust gases traveling through the EGR valve will gradually form deposits on the valve stem and in its passages. Like the sludge in the PCV system, these deposits begin to restrict and then plug the EGR valve, preventing valve stem movement. When an EGR valve sticks in a closed position, it has no effect on engine operation. It simply increases the amount of NOX emitted from the tailpipe. But if the EGR valve sticks in a partial or open position, the exhaust gases will reach the intake manifold whenever the engine is running. This results in a rough idle and poor low-speed operation.

Testing the operation of your EGR valve is fairly simple in most cases, although its location is such that you'll have to use a small mirror to watch the movement of the valve stem. You may even find it easier to monitor the valve stem movement if you remove the air cleaner housing from the carburetor. Warm the engine up to normal operating temperature (195 degrees F.) and let it idle. Connect a vacuum gauge between the EGR valve and the carburetor. Watch the valve stem closely as you open the throttle until the gauge reads at least 5 inches of vacuum; then close the throttle. The valve stem should move about ⅛ inch, or enough to open and close the valve as you open/close the throttle. If the stem does not move, the chances are good that deposits inside the valve are restricting its operation.

buretor. If the PCV valve becomes plugged or otherwise restricted, the system operates as described at all times. This makes the air cleaner housing a dumping ground for the same kind of gluck that will plug or restrict your PCV valve.

The PCV system is the easiest emissions system to test and service. Simply pull the valve out of the rocker cover with the engine running at idle. Place your thumb over the end of the valve and you should feel suction. If there is no vacuum, either the valve or the hoses are plugged. When the engine is shut off, shake the valve vigorously and listen for a clicking noise inside. If you cannot hear a noise, replace the valve with a new one.

PCV valves are replacement items. They cannot be disassembled and cleaned. Many mechanics, however, will shoot a squirt of carburetor cleaner or another solvent into the PCV valve and stuff it back into the rocker cover. This amounts to nothing if the valve is already partially restricted, but if you do this with a new PCV valve every time you tune the engine, it will help delay formation of the sludge that inevitably ends up in the valve.

If you totally ignore the PCV system for many thousands of miles, one of the hoses may become partially restricted or even totally plugged with the crankcase gluck. Should this be the case, don't even try to clean the hose—throw it away and install a new one. But don't think that just any old hose will do—the one you use must be designed to resist the destructive action of crankcase vapors or it will rot almost immediately. If blow-by gases can literally eat away engine bearings (and they can), a piece of untreated hose won't last very long once subjected to such powerful vapors.

What symptoms will tell you that the PCV system is not working properly? If the valve clogs, you'll encounter engine stalling, a rough idle, and/or engine overheating. If you let it go long enough, a plugged PCV valve will cause gasket leaks, bearing failure, scuffed pistons, and even burned valves and spark plugs.

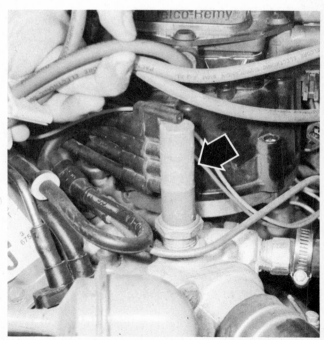
You'll find these funny-looking devices scattered around the engine—this is the DS/Canister Purge Thermal Vacuum Switch (arrow).

Emissions Controls

The EGR system as used on X-cars is temperature-controlled by a thermal vacuum switch (TVS) which senses engine coolant temperature. To determine whether the EGR valve or the EGR-TVS switch is at fault, trace the vacuum line which carries the signal from the switch to the EGR valve and disconnect it at the switch. With the engine running, connect a vacuum gauge and partially open the throttle. The vacuum gauge should show an increased reading. If it doesn't, remove the switch hose which connects to the carburetor. Hook the vacuum gauge to this hose so that you're picking up the signal directly from the carburetor. Partially open the throttle again, and if the gauge reading increases, replace the TVS. If the gauge doesn't respond, the switch is okay. Look instead for a plugged hose or a restriction in the carburetor vacuum passage.

EGR valves are very expensive these days, so you might be tempted to try and clean them up to avoid

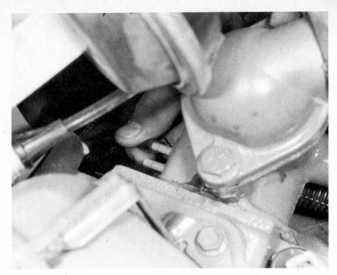

Locating some of the TVS switches on either engine is a matter of using the vacuum hose diagram on the decal and tracing the lines. This one is located behind the L4 thermostat port.

A thermal vacuum switch, or TVS, looks like this when removed from the engine or radiator. One port connects to a vacuum source. Heat applied to the end of the TVS opens/closes passages leading to the other ports to control vacuum flow.

purchasing new ones. This is not a good idea. If the deposits are sufficient to restrict valve stem movement, they'll be too difficult to remove. The deposits are rock-hard and cannot be dissolved by solvents. You'll have to scrape them off by hand, and it's possible to damage the valve stem while you're trying to clean it. Stay ahead of the game and install a new valve.

Make sure you replace the old valve with a new one which bears the same part number. The X-car EGR systems use three different EGR valves: the standard vacuum-modulated valve, a negative backpressure-modulated valve, and a positive backpressure-modulated valve. Either take the old valve with you when you buy the replacement or be sure and copy all the numbers to help the parts department determine the exact replacement valve you need.

Pulsair Injection Reactor (Pair) System

This is an air injection system which supplies fresh air to the exhaust ports where it mixes with the hot exhaust gases and ignites. Since this afterburning effect turns unburned hydrocarbons (HC) into harmless water vapor, it works to reduce exhaust emissions. Unlike other air injection systems which use a belt-driven air pump, the Pulsair system uses a series of distribution pipes and check valves which depend upon the engine's exhaust pulses to draw air into the exhaust system. Air from the Pulsair system is injected into the exhaust port near the exhaust valve.

What can go wrong with the Pulsair system? Well, except for distribution hose leaks and air valve failures, not very much. You can test the air valve operation with a hand vacuum pump. Disconnect the Pulsair line at the air valve fitting and connect the pump directly to the valve. If you have the V6 engine, disconnect both Pulsair valves and test each one individually. Draw 15 inches of vacuum and clock how long it takes the vacuum level to drop to 5 inches. If the vacuum drop occurs in two seconds or less, replace the valve.

Evaporative Emissions System

This system was covered in some detail in the Fuel Systems chapter, but if your engine is hard to start when it's hot, you might check the vapor canister. The vent and purge lines between the carburetor and the canister should both take a downhill route, free from any dips or bends. If one or both lines have a kink or sag, the vapors traveling from the canister may condense. This forms solid fuel in the line and will cause hard starting when the engine is hot. Trying to troubleshoot this one can drive you close to the brink—but don't let someone sell you a new starter if this condition occasionally develops—check it out first.

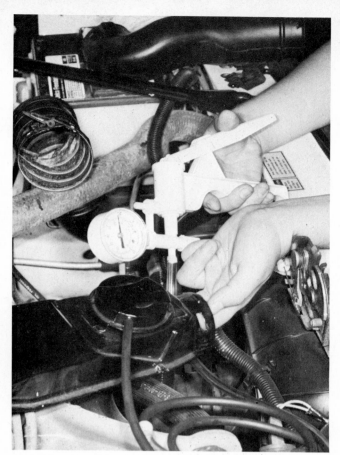

Thermac door operation is important to good driveability. Check door operation by applying a vacuum to the snorkel motor to see if the door moves.

Vacuum Delay Valves

These are usually two-colored circular plastic wafers found in vacuum lines under the hood. Fitted with a connecting nipple on each end, they contain a restriction which slows or delays a vacuum signal to modify the operation of some component. The most common, of course, are those installed in the vacuum line between the carburetor and distributor. These modify the distributor vacuum advance operation. Some are tied in with the EGR system and others operate in conjunction with a coolant temperature switch.

To know what each one does and whether it's doing its job correctly requires the knowledge of someone who's completely familiar with the X-car emissions system. This may leave out many owners, but if you have a hand vacuum pump and know the specifications for each valve in the various systems, you can check them periodically with the pump to see if they're working correctly. If not, they can be replaced quite easily. The color-coding relates to the delay duration. Your dealer can tell you the exact specifications for the valves installed under your hood.

If you find it necessary to remove a delay or check valve from the vacuum line, or even remove the entire line connecting two components, make sure that the valve (or the lines) is installed so that it faces in the correct direction. Many delay valves have raised letters stamped on them to indicate the proper direction in which they must fit into the vacuum line. For example, one installed in the distributor-to-carburetor vacuum line may read DIST on one side and CARB on the other. Replace the valve incorrectly and it will not do its job. When this happens, the driveability of your X-car will suffer.

The problem generally develops after someone has disconnected the lines, either at the carburetor or at the canister. It's also possible that the lines were mixed up when they were reconnected. If you find it necessary to remove the lines, be sure to follow the vacuum line routing diagram in the engine compartment when you reconnect them.

The canister uses a replaceable filter which GM recommends be changed every 30,000 miles. Fresh air passing through the filter forces the vapor into the purge line, where it passes to the carburetor. A dirty filter will reduce the amount of air available to purge the canister and results in poor driveability. See that your canister is serviced at least at the factory-specified intervals, if not sooner.

Should you lose your gas tank cap, don't drive around with a paper or piece of cloth stuffed in the tank's filler tube. This practice is not only dangerous, it defeats the purpose of the evaporative emissions system. Gas tank caps are calibrated according to the system, so you shouldn't install just any old cap that happens to fit.

Today's sealed fuel supply systems use a cap containing vacuum and pressure release valves. If you install a cap without such valves, you'll encounter vapor lock problems. When excessive pressure builds up in the fuel system on a hot day, the end result can be a damaged fuel tank and another set of dangerous circumstances. Use the proper gas cap only.

You can't clean a PCV valve, but a few squirts of carburetor cleaner now and then will reduce sludge buildup.

Emissions Controls

Vacuum Lines

Keep a close eye on the vacuum lines and hoses under the hood; they must be kept in good condition. As long as the system can transmit vacuum without a leak, everything is okay. But once a leak develops somewhere in the system, you'll begin to experience problems in driveability and starting which can be difficult to troubleshoot.

Inspect the lines and hoses whenever you tune the engine. They have a tendency to harden with age, turn brittle because of the high under-hood temperature, and crack from vibration. Like cooling system hoses, replace them before they fail. It's a good idea to keep a few lengths of the appropriate size and type of vacuum line on hand so that you can install new lines whenever the old ones require replacement.

The vapor canister is tucked away under several hoses at the left front of the engine compartment. Proper hose connection and routing are necessary for good driveability.

These two switches monitor the engine vacuum and signal the throttle position to the ECM on C-4-equipped L4 engines.

Early Fuel Evaporation Valve

The V6 engine has a heat control or heat riser valve installed between the exhaust manifold and the exhaust pipe leading to the catalytic converter. A vacuum diaphragm mounted on the exhaust manifold is mechanically linked to the heat control valve shaft. Vacuum control is used to provide better evaporation and distribution of the air/fuel mixture.

The heat valve is held in a closed position by both a weight and a spring. The spring relaxes as the exhaust heats up because not as much heat is needed under the carburetor when the engine is warm. The weight is offset so that it has a tendency to hold the valve in a closed position, but the valve itself is also offset on the shaft so that any excess rush of exhaust gases will have a tendency to open it. A combination of these factors results in an exhaust heat valve that forces the right amount of exhaust gas through the heating passages in the intake manifold so that the engine will operate without a stumble. It

also assures sufficient vaporization of the gasoline to get good mileage.

A thermal vacuum switch allows vacuum to reach the EFE valve diaphragm during start-up when coolant temperature is low. The diaphragm pulls the lever to close the heat control valve. As the engine warms up, the coolant temperature closes the TVS, blocking vacuum to the diaphragm. The diaphragm then returns to normal and pulls the heat control valve open to let exhaust gas flow through.

If the car is only driven short distances at a time and thus never completely warms up, the EFE valve may give problems. The heavy condensation of moisture while the engine is cold, plus the extra carbon caused by the engine running "rich" on a partial choke setting, may combine to freeze the shaft of the EFE valve in a closed position.

Once rust and carbon have a good grip on the EFE valve, all the high-speed driving you want to do will not free it. Exhaust gases must pass through the EFE valve passages of the intake manifold, thus providing an oversupply of heat to the base of the carburetor, making vapor lock a major problem. You can prevent this by periodic inspection and lubrication of the EFE valve shaft. Your GM dealer uses a special manifold valve lubricant, and this should be used instead of engine oil, WD-40, or other general-purpose lubricants. It's specially formulated to resist formation of the carbon and exhaust deposit buildup, and if used often enough, you'll have no EFE valve problems.

You should also check the vacuum diaphragm operation with a hand vacuum pump at the same time you lubricate the EFE valve shaft. "T" the vacuum pump into the EFE valve vacuum line. Draw 8 to 10 inches of vacuum and the valve should close. Hold the vacuum for 60 seconds. The valve should not leak down more than 2 inches of vacuum in this time and should return to the open position when

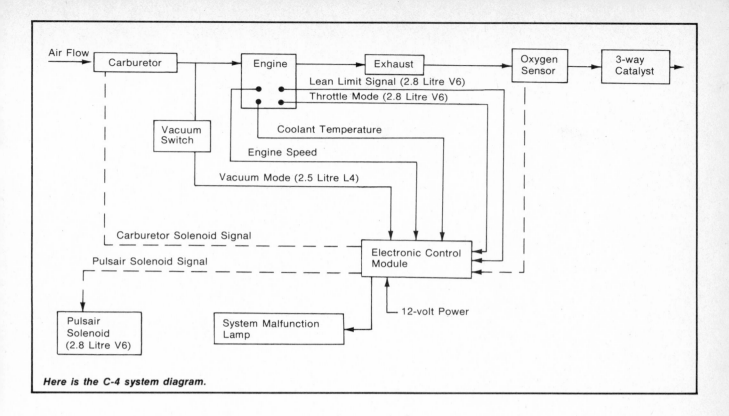

Here is the C-4 system diagram.

you vent the vacuum. If the valve does not open, replace the diaphragm assembly.

Start the engine and warm it to normal operating temperature. The EFE valve should now open. If it does not, disconnect the vacuum line to the diaphragm. The valve should open at this point, indicating a faulty diaphragm air bleed, TVS, or thermostat.

Deceleration Valve

A deceleration or decel valve is used on all X-car engines to prevent backfiring when you back off the throttle suddenly. The valve is located between the fresh-air intake and the intake manifold, and bleeds additional air to lean the air/fuel mixture during periods of high manifold vacuum, such as deceleration. A built-in check valve is used to offset the decrease in vacuum caused by sudden acceleration. You can tell a faulty decel valve by a rough idle/backfire condition.

Catalytic Converter

The catalytic converter is installed between the exhaust manifold and muffler in the exhaust system. This oxidizes unburned HC and CO emissions in the exhaust before they reach the tailpipe and pass into the atmosphere to form smog. There's nothing you can do to maintain the catalytic converter other than to use unleaded gasoline as required (leaded gas neutralizes the catalyst) and periodically check the converter housing and heat shields for dents/damage.

The converter used with the V6 engine requires a catalyst change at 30,000 miles, as indicated by a red flag which will appear on the instrument panel. Installing a new converter is much like replacing

a muffler. If you wish to do the job yourself, you should have no major problems as long as you have the proper tools. It's not advisable, however, to attempt to change the catalyst in the housing yourself. This requires specialized equipment and should be done by your dealer. California models for 1980 and all 1981 X-cars using the C-4 emissions system use a special three-way converter.

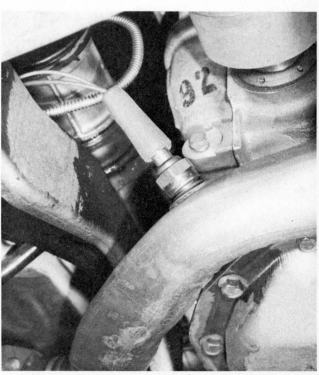

The C-4 oxygen sensor is installed in the manifold pipe on V6 engines and is removed from underneath the car.

Emissions Controls

Computer Controlled Catalytic Converter (C-4) System

Often called a closed-loop carburetion system, the C-4 uses an electronic control module, an exhaust gas oxygen sensor in the exhaust manifold, a feedback carburetor, and a three-way catalytic converter. Under normal driving circumstances, the sensor tells the module how much oxygen the exhaust gas contains, and the module signals the carburetor to adjust the air/fuel ratio accordingly. This carburetor adjustment is a continuing process, but signals from other sensors modify the module signal according to engine temperature, engine vacuum, throttle position, and engine speed. A three-way catalytic converter reduces NOx, as well as HC and CO emissions.

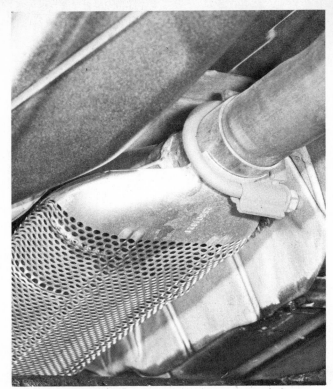

C-4-equipped cars use a three-way or dual-bed converter protected by a heat shield.

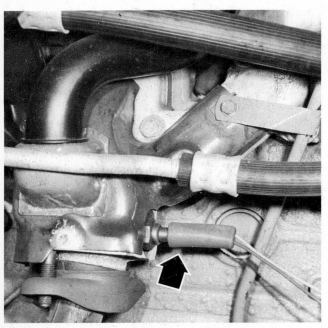

The C-4 oxygen sensor on L4 cars is installed in the manifold at the bottom of the heat stove (arrow).

It's a complicated system for the non-professional mechanic, but GM has built in a self-diagnostic testing system to help narrow down the possibilities when troubleshooting a malfunction. When certain problems occur, a "CHECK ENGINE" light appears on the instrument panel. To determine the problem, a "TROUBLE CODE" test wire under the dash is grounded, causing the CHECK ENGINE lamp to flash a numerical code.

To read the code, the engine must be running and the TROUBLE CODE test lead grounded. The CHECK ENGINE light will then flash a code, such as 14. This consists of a single flash followed by a pause and then four more flashes. The entire trouble code will be repeated three times. Once you've determined the particular test code, you must refer to a corresponding diagnosis chart to troubleshoot the specific part of the system indicated by the trouble code.

The C-4 system used on 1980 X-cars comes from the factory with a "temporary" memory. That is, a problem which develops while the car is running will place a trouble code in the module memory bank where it will remain until the ignition is turned off. Generally, the trouble code can be retrieved by restarting the engine and letting it run for a few minutes, as the problem will reappear. If it's an intermittent problem, however, the chances of retrieving the trouble code are slight. The car will have to be driven with the test lead grounded until the intermittent problem reappears; then the code can be read.

You can switch the module's memory bank from

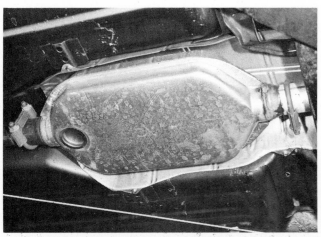

X-cars not equipped with the C-4 use the pellet-type catalytic converter.

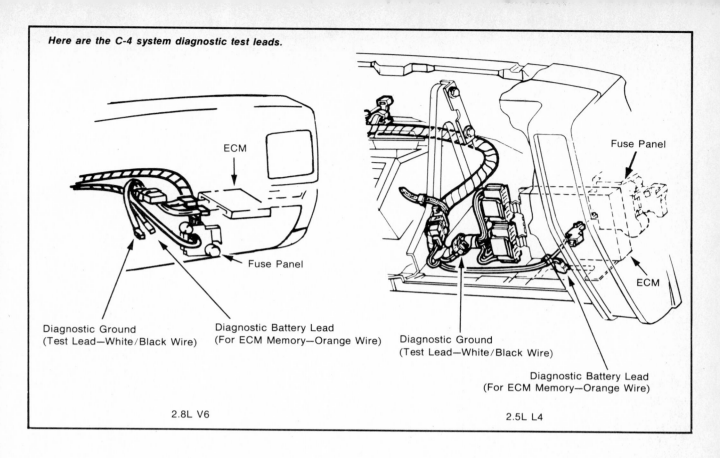

ECM

Fuse Panel

Fuse Panel

ECM

Diagnostic Ground
(Test Lead—White/Black Wire)

Diagnostic Battery Lead
(For ECM Memory—Orange Wire)

Diagnostic Ground
(Test Lead—White/Black Wire)

Diagnostic Battery Lead
(For ECM Memory—Orange Wire)

2.8L V6

2.5L L4

temporary to long-term by connecting the orange diagnostic battery lead running from the module's "S" terminal to the fuse block cavity marked "GAUGES." This allows the module to remember *any* problem, but it also causes a constant drain on the battery—even when the ignition is off. If you fail to drive the car for a few days, the drain will run down the battery. To prevent such battery damage, the orange lead should be disconnected once the problem has been determined and corrected. This also erases the trouble code from the module memory bank.

The C-4 system as used on 1981 and later models is more complex, since it controls several ignition and transmission functions in addition to monitoring and correcting the air/fuel ratio. The system is bound to grow more complicated with each passing model year, as more and more operations fall under the control of electronics.

Do it Yourself?

This discussion covers the emissions control systems which are easily understood and can be checked and maintained by almost any driver. The C-4 system is considerably more complex than our brief coverage indicates. To service it properly and efficiently requires a well-grounded background in how it works. For most of us, this means taking the car to a competent mechanic for troubleshooting and servicing when necessary. If you don't understand what you're doing, fooling around with the complex systems usually aggravates the problem or creates another. Your GM dealer is the man to see in such cases.

The V6 engine uses an EFE valve located between the exhaust manifold and exhaust pipe. This vacuum-operated butterfly increases exhaust gas flow under the intake manifold during cold engine operation.

8

The Cooling System

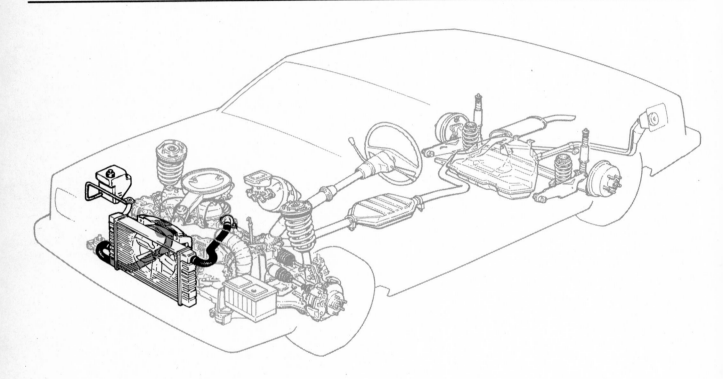

The basic X-car cooling system consists of the radiator and cap, coolant recovery reservoir, two hoses connecting the radiator to the water pump and engine, smaller hoses leading back to the firewall for the heater, a thermostat, and an electric cooling fan. All models use a crossflow radiator, which contains horizontal tubes through which the coolant circulates. A header tank is located at each side of the core. On automatic transaxle-equipped X-cars, an oil cooler or heat exchanger is built into the left tank. Inlet/outlet fittings are provided to connect the transaxle for fluid circulation.

If the cooling system is not periodically maintained, gradual deterioration takes place. One of the first things to wear out will be the radiator hoses. Not only are these subjected to the high temperatures and pressure of the coolant circulating through them, but engine compartment heat bakes their exterior. GM recommends that the hoses be

changed every 24,000 miles, and it's a good recommendation to follow, even though the hoses may *appear* to be good.

A pressure-vent cap on the radiator allows the system to operate at 15 psi, raising the coolant boiling point to approximately 262 degrees F. at sea level. The radiator cap is designed to discourage removal—always check and add coolant at the see-through recovery reservoir. However, it's a good idea to periodically check the securing lugs on the cap, as well as the internal seal and the radiator filler neck. If any of these surfaces are dented or bent, they will not make a perfect seal with the cap gasket.

Check and Correct

Keep two rules uppermost in your mind when dealing with the cooling system. First, always keep antifreeze in the cooling system. Glycol

To protect against corrosion and coolant loss due to boiling, coolant should provide freeze protection to -34 degrees F. Check the concentration with a cooling system tester.

The most important cooling system preventive maintenance operation you can perform is to inspect the hoses regularly. Squeeze them and watch for leaks. If the hoses feel swollen, soft, or mushy, it's time to replace them. Check the hose clamps and tighten if necessary every time you inspect the system. Leaks can occur in a great many places besides the hose connections. Be sure to check the heater fittings where the hoses connect to the block and water pump. Check the radiator closely, looking for rusted or corroded areas around the header tanks and at the hose connections.

Keep the radiator free of bugs, leaves, and other debris. Removing the grille (an easy job) will allow you free access to clean the cooling fins. While checking for leaks, be sure to inspect the fan belt condition and tension. The belt should be kept tight and free from defects of any kind.

Troubleshooting

The accompanying chart provides a near-complete diagnosis and cure for almost all cooling system problems. Keep it handy and learn how to troubleshoot the system. For example, if your X-car overheats, the first thing to check is coolant circulation. Remove the radiator cap when the engine is cool and fill the system until you can see coolant in the filler neck. Place a newspaper or blanket in front of the radiator and run the engine at a fast idle until it reaches operating temperature, watching the warning light or temperature gauge. Coolant should start to flow as the engine heats up, and you'll see turbulence in the filler neck. If the engine heats up and no circulation is apparent, go to the thermostat.

The temperature-operated valve prevents coolant from circulating until the engine reaches operating temperature. At that time, the thermostat opens and controls the flow of coolant to maintain a proper engine operating temperature. If this valve malfunctions in a closed position, no coolant will flow and an overheated condition results. If it fails in the open position, the engine will never get up to operating temperature and there will be no warning from the light. If you have a temperature gauge, it will read low.

serves several purposes in addition to lowering the freezing point and raising the boiling point of water. It's a wetting agent which improves heat transfer, acts as a rust and corrosion inhibitor, and contains a water pump lubricant.

Second, never try to take the cap off a hot engine. If the coolant temperature is above 212 degrees F., releasing the pressure will cause it to boil immediately—sending up a geyser of very hot steam and water that can cause a nasty burn.

There are two ways to safely reduce the pressure if you must remove the cap from a hot radiator. Cover the cap with a heavy cloth, press down on it and slowly turn to the first notch. This releases the pressure seal and lets the coolant boil off through the overflow tube to the recovery tank. A safer way is to spray the radiator core with cold water. This will reduce both the temperature and the pressure inside the radiator. When refilling the radiator with fresh coolant, keep the engine running to reduce the shock of cold liquid entering the engine block.

Whenever you remove the radiator cap, check it carefully for damage, deformity, or dried-out gaskets.

If the cooling system cannot maintain a steady 15 psi pressure, there's a leak somewhere. A cooling system pressure test will help locate the problem.

The Cooling System

The thermostat is enclosed in a housing where the upper radiator hose connects to the engine. Drain the system's fluid down to a level below the thermostat (the radiator draincock is located at the bottom of the right-hand header tank). Unbolt the housing, and remove the thermostat. To check a closed valve, place it in a pan of boiling water. It should open completely. If it fails to open, or opens only partially, replace it with a new valve of the *same* temperature rating, which can be found on the bottom or flange of each thermostat.

You can test thermostat operation by heating a pan of water and noting the temperature at which it opens/closes.

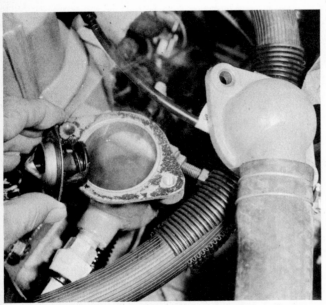

Thermostat removal is easy. Drain the coolant below the hose level and unbolt the housing.

To check circulation flow, leave the thermostat out and run the engine at a fast idle while watching the filler tube. If the coolant backs up quickly and overflows, there's a blockage in the radiator core. Remove the upper and lower radiator hoses, wrap a rag around the end of a garden hose and stick it into the lower hose connection at the radiator. Turn the water on all the way. This gives you an indication of the rate of flow through the radiator. At the same time, it will backflush the core to remove any debris that may have collected in the tanks and blocked the radiator tubes. If the water flow is restricted, you'll have to remove the radiator and take it to a radiator shop, where they will remove the tanks and "rod out" the core by passing small rods through the tubes to knock out the debris, rust, and scale. Don't be too surprised if subsequent pressure testing reveals a few leaks that will have to be repaired. One good way to prevent all this misery is to change coolant every year—antifreeze and its additives wear out.

When you refill the radiator, follow the antifreeze-to-water ratio chart if you live in a climate where below-freezing temperatures are common. Otherwise, use a 50/50 ratio and make certain to use soft water. If you don't have soft water in your locality, buy bottled mineral-free water. It's easier to use tap water, but remember that when you do, you're adding the basic ingredients that form scale and attack the additives.

On the Road

What should you do if the warning light or temperature gauge begins to flicker on or climb while you're driving? Since you only have a few degrees to go at this point before the engine coolant begins to boil, make a dash for it, if you're going uphill and are close to the summit. Otherwise, unload the engine. Pull over and park, but don't turn off the engine or the coolant will boil instantly.

Instead, run the engine at a fast idle in Neutral until the temperature comes down. Turn off the air conditioner—it puts an unnecessary load on the engine. If necessary, turn on the heater and open all the windows. Since the heater is really a small radiator, you'll increase your engine-cooling capacity by this much extra.

Such problems can be avoided by following the simple preventive maintenance procedures we've outlined. Pay attention to the cooling system, and you'll have no roadside emergencies.

Cooling system switches have you confused? "A" controls the dash indicator lamp, "B" works in conjunction with the air conditioning, and "C" is a sensor for the electronic control module. The V6 uses the same switches, but in different locations.

COOLING SYSTEM DIAGNOSIS

Complaint	Possible Cause	Correction
Coolant Loss	Pressure cap and gasket	Inspect, wash gasket, and test. Replace only if cap will not hold pressure test specification of 15 psi.
	Leakage	Pressure test system.
	–External	Inspect hose, hose connection, radiator, engine core plugs and drain plugs, transaxle oil cooler lines, water pump, heater component lines. Repair or replace as necessary.
	–Internal	Disassemble engine as required. Check for cracked intake manifold, blown head gasket, warped head/block gasket surfaces, cracked cylinder head or engine block.
Engine Overheats	Low coolant level	Fill as required. Check for coolant loss.
	Loose fan belt	Adjust tension.
	Pressure cap	Test. Replace if necessary.
	Radiator or A/C condenser obstruction	Remove debris, leaves, bugs, etc.
	Stuck thermostat (closed)	Test. Replace if necessary.
	Electric fan failure	Test. Replace if necessary.
	Ignition	Check timing and advance. Adjust as required.
	Temperature gauge/warning light	Check electrical circuits and repair as required.
Engine Fails To Reach Normal Operating Temperature	Open thermostat	Test. Replace if necessary.
	Temperature gauge/warning light	Check electrical circuits and repair as required.

The Electric Cooling Fan

In cars with a traditional front-to-rear engine mounting, airflow through the radiator is provided by an engine-driven fan attached to the end of the water pump shaft. When the engine is shut off, the fan stops working. X-cars, however, have a transverse-mounted engine and cannot use a water pump/cooling fan arrangement. To provide airflow through the radiator, a 12-inch fan with five plastic blades is mounted to the radiator support and driven by a small electric motor.

The fan is operated by a relay mounted at the front of the engine compartment on the passenger side. The relay contacts have voltage available constantly, while the relay coil receives voltage through the C/H fuse only when the ignition switch is in the "RUN" position. A coolant temperature switch (CTS) controls current flow and is normally open. When engine coolant temperature reaches 230 degrees F., the CTS closes and the fan operates. A drop in coolant temperature below 214 degrees F. closes the switch and the fan stops. Air conditioned cars also have a second CTS in the circuit to activate the fan whenever compressor refrigerant pressure exceeds 1790 kPa/260 psi.

Shutting off the engine will not stop the fan—it will continue to run until the coolant temperature drops below the CTS activation level. You should be extra careful when working under the hood with the engine running, as the cooling fan may start up unexpectedly. If your fingers are in the way, or test equipment leads dangle in the fan's path, serious injury or damage can occur.

If the cooling fan doesn't run, check the C/H fuse in the fuse box first. If the fuse is good, check the fusible link at the relay. Ground the relay coil by connecting a jumper between the dark green/white wire at the relay and a good engine ground, and the fan should run. When the fan does not stop, you've got a problem with either the temperature or pressure switch.

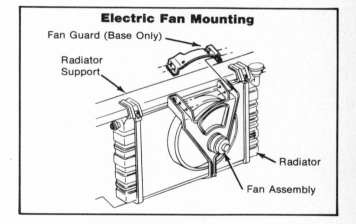

Electric Fan Mounting

Fan Guard (Base Only)
Radiator Support
Radiator
Fan Assembly

The cooling fan relay is mounted at the front of the engine compartment above the right-hand headlamp. This controls operation of the electric fan.

9

The Brake System

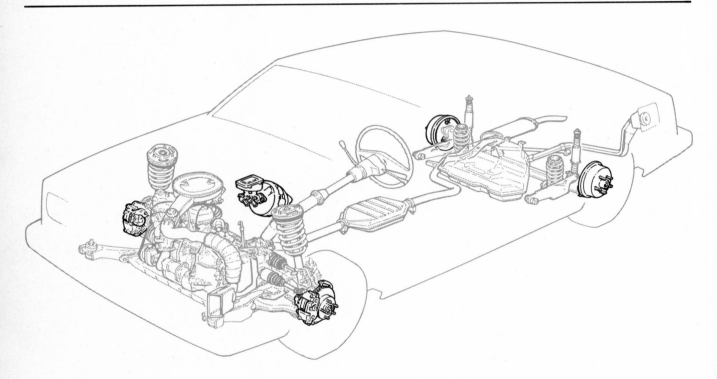

The elementary principle that fluids cannot be compressed determines how your brakes work. Thus, it's possible to move a column of hydraulic fluid (liquid) from the storage container (master cylinder) through tubing (brake lines) to the slave or wheel cylinders by means of pressure. Movement at the wheel cylinders causes the brake lining (a friction material) to come into contact with the wheel-driven drum or disc rotor, forcing it to slow down or to stop completely.

Filled with hydraulic fluid, the master cylinder contains a piston with its connecting rod linkage. Activation of the master cylinder piston via the connecting rod linkage pushes brake fluid through the brake lines to each wheel cylinder. The wheel cylinder pistons, in turn, push outward to force the brake shoes against the revolving drum. As this pressure should be equal at all wheel cylinders, effective braking pressure cannot be applied to any one

wheel until all the shoes on the wheels are in contact with their respective drums. This provides a self-equalizing effect.

While liquids cannot be compressed, gases such as air can be. For this reason, it's very important to keep the hydraulic system free of air bubbles. Removing such air is done by "bleeding" the brakes, an important and necessary part of any brake system servicing. To help ensure that the system is always free of air, rubber or neoprene cuplike seals are used on all cylinders, and a fluid supply reservoir is built into the master cylinder.

Especially compounded for automotive hydraulic brake systems, brake fluid withstands very low temperatures without freezing and very high temperatures without boiling away. There are, however, some precautions that should be observed. Brake fluid should never be mixed with, or contaminated by, solvents; exposed to air, which will cause it to

Driving on worn-out pads will score the rotor surface. If this happens, it should be resurfaced, unless the new thickness will be less than the specified minimum. A special lathe is used to machine the rotor. The strap placed around the rotor dampens vibration.

become sticky; or allowed to contact brake lining material, which will ruin the material.

Besides the self-equalizing feature and the elimination of mechanical linkage from the pedal to the wheels, hydraulic systems multiply force and create leverage. If you apply a pedal force of 100 pounds—which is not difficult to exert under a panic-stop condition—hydraulic line pressure may range between 800 and 1300 psi. Despite the rather long travel of the brake pedal when applied, the wheel cylinder pistons and brake shoes don't have to move very far to touch the drum because of the mechanical and hydraulic leverage.

The X-Car Braking System

Now that we know something about the hydraulics involved, let's look at the X-car system. All X-cars use a diagonal split hydraulic brake system. The master cylinder contains two individual pressure circuits. The primary circuit (front of the master cylinder) activates one front brake and its opposite at the rear. The secondary circuit (rear of cylinder) operates the other front and opposing rear brake. If power-assist is provided, the master cylinder is attached to a vacuum booster unit. This

reduces the amount of pressure that must be applied in order to operate the brakes.

The master cylinder assembly incorporates a warning light switch and a proportioner for each circuit. A "quick take-up" valve provides a large volume of brake fluid to the wheel brakes at low pressure when the brake pedal is first applied. This low-pressure fluid compensates rapidly for the displacement of fluid when the caliper pistons and brake shoe springs retract.

Brake Adjustment

The sliding action of the disc brake caliper automatically compensates for pad wear. The rear brakes adjust themselves whenever the car is moving backward with the brake pedal firmly applied. A brake adjustment slot is also provided on the drum. This is used to remove tension on the shoes when you're pulling the drums, and to readjust the linings when the drum is replaced.

If the brakes have never been adjusted, you'll probably have to punch out the adjustment hole. Locate the lanced area on the drum and remove it with a punch and hammer. If there is no lanced area on the drum, drill a ½-inch hole in the round flat area on the backing plate, opposite the parking brake cable. This will permit access to the star-wheel adjuster.

To adjust the rear brakes, turn the star-wheel with a screwdriver blade or brake adjusting tool to expand the shoes until you can just barely rotate the wheel by hand. Back off the star-wheel about 30 notches at each wheel. Rotate the wheel by hand. If there is still a light drag, back the star-wheel off

Whenever you work on the disc brakes, always remove some of the fluid in the master cylinder reservoir. This lets you compress the caliper piston without causing the reservoir to overflow.

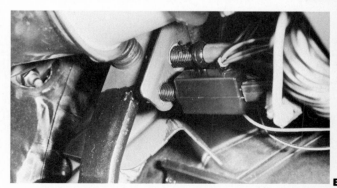

The stoplight switch configuration differs according to how the car is equipped. The switch in (A) is found on manual transmission cars; the one in (B) is used on cars with an automatic transmission and cruise control.

The Brake System

another notch or two. Install an adjusting hole cover in the slot to keep dirt and moisture out. These can be obtained from any GM dealer if your car is not equipped with them.

Once you've adjusted the rear brakes satisfactorily, be sure to check the parking brake adjustment. Depress the parking brake pedal exactly two notches or ratchet clicks; tighten the adjusting nut at the equalizer until you can just barely rotate the left rear wheel backward, but not forward, with both hands; release the parking brake; and both rear wheels should turn freely with no drag in either direction.

X-car disc brakes have a built-in wear indicator designed to alert the driver when the pads need replacement.

Bleeding the System

Once you've finished working on the braking system, it must be bled. This is the only sure way to rid the lines of any air that might have entered them. You can bleed the brakes without special equipment, but you'll need the help of a friend to operate the brake pedal while you work at the wheel. Since the two brake systems are separate, bleed them separately.

Fill the brake fluid reservoir with brake fluid. Don't let it run dry or air will enter the lines and you'll have to rebleed them. Clean the bleed valve at each wheel, then connect a length of tubing to the valve at one wheel. Place the other end in a container with sufficient fresh brake fluid to cover the end of the hose. As you open the bleed valve, have your friend depress the pedal slowly until it reaches the bottom of its travel. Close the valve just before the pedal bottoms out and then have your friend let the pedal return to its normal position.

Continue the process until the fluid stream from the hose is free from air bubbles, then close the valve and remove the hose. Refill the brake fluid reservoir each time and repeat the process at each wheel. After bleeding all four wheels, top up the reservoir and replace the cap.

Troubleshooting Problems

Before you decide to tackle your brakes, see if you can determine exactly where the cause of your problem is. You can do this by testing the brakes on a strip of smooth, dry pavement where traffic is nonexistent, or very light. Apply the brakes firmly for as quick a stop as possible at about 20 mph without locking the wheels. If the pedal stops a couple of inches or so from the floorboard, your linings are badly worn, the brake fluid level is too low, or the brake shoes need adjusting.

A spongy feeling to the pedal indicates air in the system. Check this out by pressing the brake pedal as hard as you can with the car stopped. Hold the pedal down firmly to see if it continues to move downward slowly. If it does, you've got a vacuum booster problem, poor sealing in the master or wheel cylinders, or a leak in the brake lines.

Several problems are indicated when the car pulls to one side or another or a wheel ''grabs'' when the brakes are applied. This can be caused by any of the following: grease or hydraulic fluid on the linings or disc pads, incorrect adjustment, a loose backing plate, shoes that don't meet the drum surfaces evenly, a plugged master cylinder relief valve, poor pedal linkage adjustment, or even an out-of-round drum.

A grinding noise or a squeak when the brakes are applied means that you should inspect the pad and shoe linings. They may be worn to the metal, or they may have acquired some oil or grease on the lining surface. A warped backing plate can cause a similar noise with the rear brakes. And don't overlook the wheel bearings. They can affect braking efficiency and cause a lot of futile searching for a defect in the brake system. X-car wheel bearings are lubricated for life and are not adjustable. If there is a problem with the wheel bearing, the bearing and hub assembly should be replaced.

Solving the Problem

If you decide to work on your brakes, pick a level, solid surface on which to jack up the wheels. A garage hoist is ideal, but you can work with the regular X-car jack and four jackstands. Block the other wheels, loosen the wheel stud nuts and raise the wheel on which you'll be working until the tire clears the ground. If you're working on the rear wheels, position a jackstand at the rear axle between the spring seats. When the front wheels are being serviced, position the stands under the cradle crossbar and lower control arm. Slowly lower the jack until the car rests securely on the stands.

Now remove the wheel/tire assembly. If you're

Valve Replacement

Early proportioning valves used on X-car master cylinders were steel; aluminum replacement valves are original equipment on later production models. If one valve is malfunctioning, both should be replaced as aluminum and steel valves should not be used together on the same master cylinder. The proper replacement valve is gold/light green in color and carries GM part No. 18006626-7. If your car is equipped with these new aluminum valves, replacement can be made either as individual units or in pairs.

working on the front disc brakes, this will give you access to the caliper and brake pads. With the rear brakes, you should back off the star-wheel adjuster to draw the shoes away from the drum. If the drum refuses to come off freely, try tapping it sharply on the sides; if it still doesn't come free, you may need the use of a brake drum puller to remove it.

Mark the shoes so that you can return them to their original position on the proper wheel if you're not going to replace them with new ones. Remove the shoes as shown in our pictorial sequence. Clean and inspect the brakes, checking the wheel cylinder for a piston leak. If there is a dark stain around the cylinder, it should be thoroughly cleaned and rebuilt.

Abnormal drum wear may cause brake problems, so be sure to check the drums. They can become out-of-round after long periods of normal use. In addition, they're almost always scored from the abrasive action of dust and dirt between the linings and the drum. If you suspect defects on the braking surface, take the drums to a garage and have the surface restored by machining on a special brake drum lathe. The maximum rebore diameter of X-car brake drums is 200.64mm.

Disc brake rotors also have a tendency to develop circular scoring. When this becomes excessive, it causes brake squeal and shortens the life of the pads. Scoring that goes beyond .015 inch cannot be removed by resurfacing. In such cases, resurfacing will make the rotor too thin for safe use. You'll have to replace the rotor with a new one.

Use a micrometer to measure rotor thickness whenever you work on the disc brakes. Take eight different measurements about ¾ inch from the outer edge and approximately 45 degrees from each other. The minimum rotor thickness (21.08mm) is cast into the rotor and should be used for comparison with your readings.

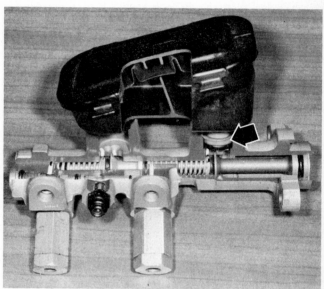

The X-car master cylinder contains two proportioner valves and a quick take-up valve assembly, making it more complex than other master cylinders.

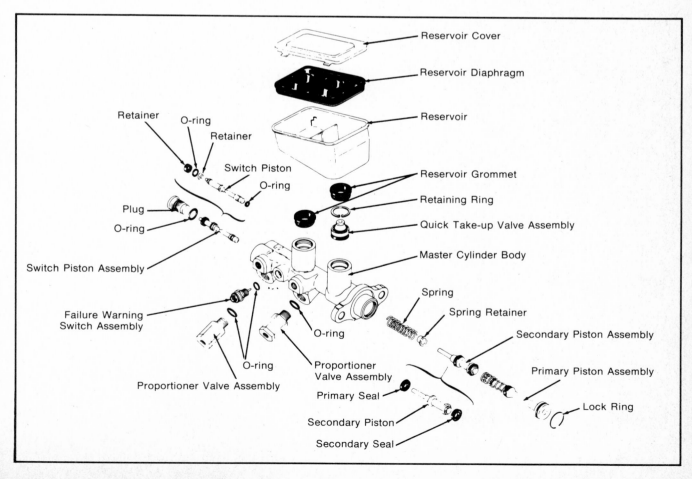

The Brake System-Master Cylinder Overhaul

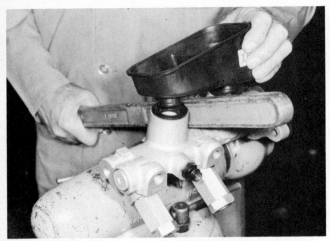

1. To disassemble the master cylinder, clamp the body ear in a vise and use a pry bar to pop the reservoir loose from housing grommets.

2. To remove the quick-take-up valve assembly, you'll have to pry the grommet from the rear reservoir bore.

3. You'll need snap-ring pliers with an angled tip in order to remove the snap ring—there's no substitute.

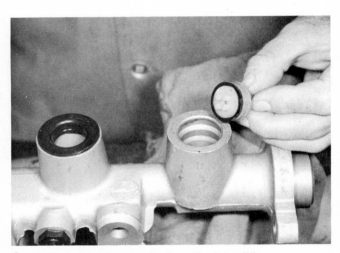

4. Lift the quick-take-up valve from the bore. When replacing, the snap ring must seat properly in the body groove.

5. Unscrew the brake failure warning switch. The original switch may or may not use an O-ring. Replacement torque value is 15-50 in.-lbs.

6. Unscrew and remove the proportioner from each brake circuit and replace the O-ring. Replacement torque value is 18-30 ft.-lbs.

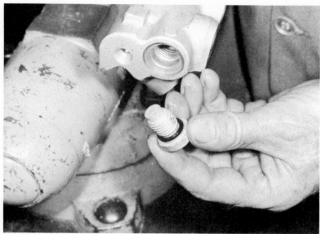

7. An Allen-head plug holds the switch piston assembly in place. Install new O-ring. Replacement torque value is 40-140 in.-lbs.

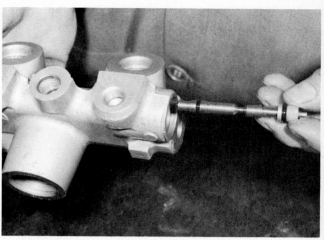

8. Remove the switch piston assembly. Install new O-rings and retainers on the piston before replacing it in the master cylinder.

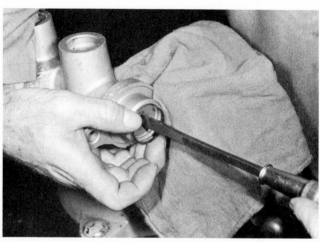

9. To remove the primary/secondary piston assemblies, depress the piston as shown and remove lock ring.

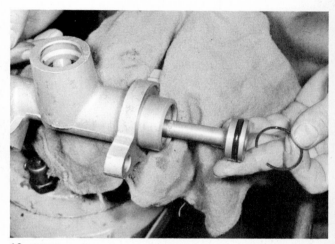

10. Withdraw the primary piston from the bore. Compressed air can be used to remove the secondary piston, but cover the bore with cloth.

11. Install new O-rings on the piston assemblies and inspect cylinder bore for corrosion. Install the secondary piston first.

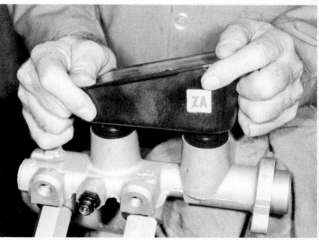

12. Use new rubber grommets when replacing the reservoir. To fit the reservoir in place easily, use a rocking motion and press down.

The Brake System-Disc Brake and Caliper Overhaul

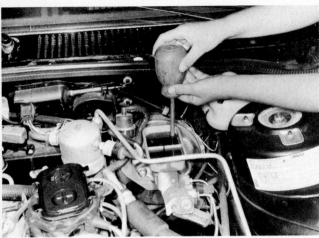

1. Before working on disc brakes, remove about two-thirds of the brake fluid from the master cylinder reservoir to prevent overflow when the caliper pistons are compressed.

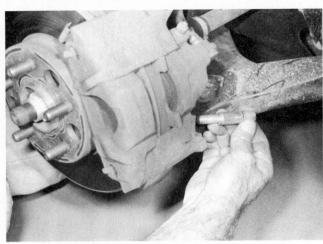

2. A 5/16-inch hex wrench is required to remove the upper and lower mounting bolts from the rear of the caliper. You'll have to tap the wrench with a hammer to loosen these bolts.

3. Grasp the caliper in both hands and work it off the rotor. There's enough slack in the brake line to permit caliper removal without disconnecting the inlet fitting.

4. The outer shoe is crimped to the caliper in two places. Support the caliper on the rotor as shown, and bend the crimped ears back with a punch and several light taps.

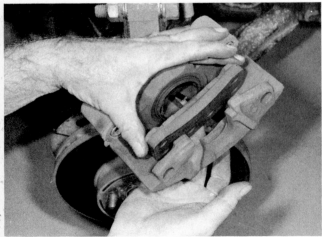

5. Pop the inboard shoe from the caliper. Note the retainer spring on the rear of the shoe. There's also a pair of retention lugs on the shoe.

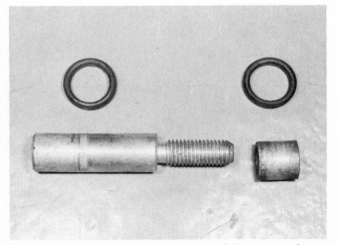

6. The caliper contains a sleeve and two O-rings on each side. Since the mounting bolt fits through these, new O-rings and sleeves should be installed each time the caliper is removed.

7. The rotor slips on and off the hub freely. Be careful not to knock it off the hub accidentally—this can damage the surface. Check the surface and if necessary, remove it for resurfacing.

8. If the caliper requires service due to leakage or sticking, disconnect inlet fitting and wash the unit in brake fluid. Blow dry with compressed air and pry the boot from the piston bore.

9. The piston can only be removed from the caliper by directing compressed air into the inlet hole. Never try to knock the piston free or pry it from the caliper bore.

10. Inspect the piston carefully for scoring, nicks, corrosion, and worn or damaged chrome plating. If any defects are found, the piston must be replaced.

11. Remove the piston seal from the caliper bore groove and inspect the bore for the same defects as with the piston. Clean the bore with crocus cloth, wipe it clean, and install a new seal in the groove.

12. Lubricate the caliper bore with clean brake fluid, attach a new dust boot to the piston, and press straight into caliper bore as shown until it's fully seated.

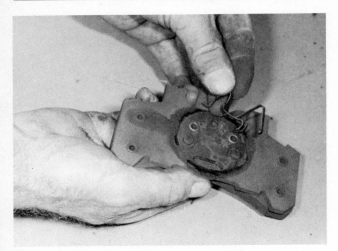

13. Unclip the shoe retainer spring from the old set of inboard pads. If the spring is deformed or bends when removed, install a new set on new inboard pads.

14. Do not touch the face of the shoe lining with greasy hands or brake fluid. Install the shoe retainer spring as shown and you're ready to reassemble the brakes.

15. Fit the new inboard shoe into the caliper and press in place so that the retainer spring fits inside the piston; then install a new outboard shoe in the caliper.

16. Push the rotor all the way on the hub, position the caliper over the rotor, and work into place. A slight wiggling motion should seat it properly on the rotor.

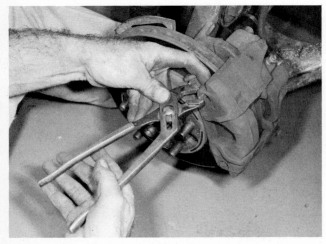

17. Using a pair of channel-lock pliers, cinch the outboard shoe ears to the caliper as shown; then install the mounting bolts at rear of caliper and thread in place finger-tight.

18. Finish tightening the mounting bolts with a hex-head wrench and tap the wrench with a hammer until bolts are snug. Remount the wheel and refill the master cylinder reservoir.

The Brake System-Drum Brake Lining Replacement

1. To service the rear brakes, support the car on jackstands and remove the wheel. The brake drum should come off easily when pulled. If it doesn't, loosen star-wheel adjuster.

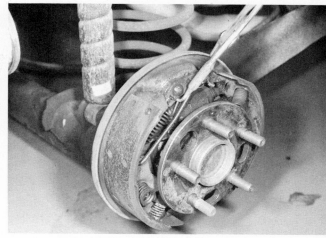

2. A set of brake tools will make service easier. Use a spring removal tool to unclip front and rear return springs from the upper assembly arm.

3. These springs are of equal length, so there should be no problem when it comes to reinstalling them. If no signs of leaking fluid are found, the wheel cylinders are okay.

4. To remove shoes from the backing plate, hold the pin from behind the plate. Grasp the hold-down spring with brake pliers, push in, and rotate it 90 degrees to free the spring.

5. The hold-down springs are different in length. The short spring is used on the rear shoe, the long one on the front shoe. You'll also find that the shoes are different in length.

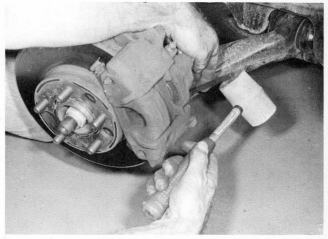

6. With the hold-down springs removed, grasp the actuator lever/pivot assembly and swing it out from behind the hub. Disengage it from the link, and then remove the link.

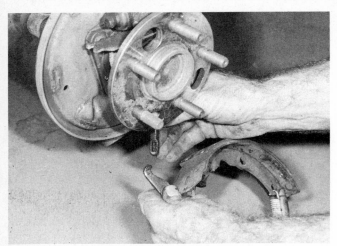

7. Grasp the shoes as an assembly and remove them from the backing plate; then swivel the assembly to remove parking brake lever from parking brake cable end.

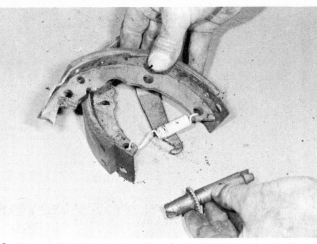

8. Disassemble the shoes, star-wheel adjuster and adjusting shoe. Remove and save the circlip which holds the parking brake lever to old shoe—circlip will be reused.

9. Clean the backing plate and wheel cylinder of brake dust; then place the parking brake strut/spring assembly between wheel cylinder and hub as shown.

10. Install the parking brake lever to the new rear shoe, and snap the circlip in place. Do not touch the new linings with greasy fingers or brake fluid.

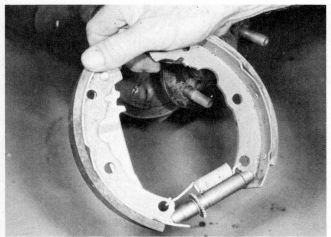

11. Carefully assemble the new shoes, star-wheel, and adjusting spring as shown. If the adjusting spring is installed upside down, it will prevent adjuster operation.

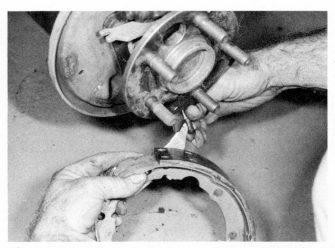

12. Swivel the lining assembly to connect the parking brake lever to the cable end; then rotate the assembly right-side up in position to install it on the backing plate.

13. Spread the lining assembly and fit it over the hub. Seat it on the backing plate and engage the parking brake strut with each shoe, fitting the shoe ends against the wheel cylinder pistons.

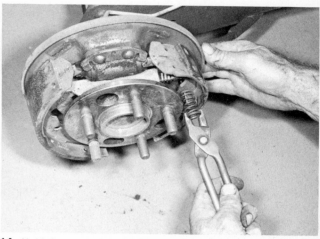

14. Hold the assembly in place and install the hold-down pin from the rear of backing plate. Hold the pin in place and install the long hold-down spring, turning it 90 degrees to lock it in place.

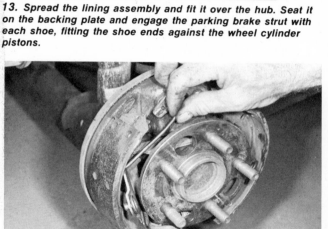

15. Attach the actuating link to the actuator lever/pivot assembly and install behind the hub. The pivot and spring should hold the lever in place for the next step.

16. With the actuator assembly in position, install the hold-down pin through the backing plate and fasten the hold-down spring. Check to see that the shoes and actuator are properly assembled.

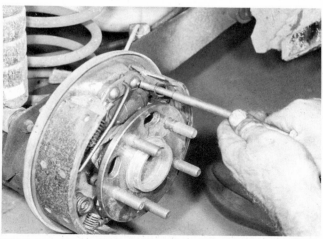

17. Connect the return springs to the brake shoes. Expand the springs with a brake tool to attach the spring end to the upper arm. This completes the installation of the new linings.

18. Turn the star-wheel adjuster with channel-lock pliers to adjust the brake before replacing the drum. Remount the wheel, and the brake job is done. Back the car up and the self-adjuster will take over.

10

Clutch and Manual Transaxle

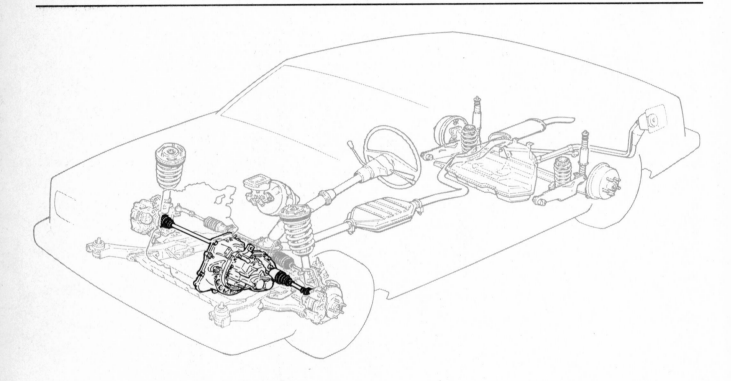

The engine alone in your X-car can't develop any appreciable torque at low speeds. It can develop its maximum torque only at one relatively high speed. In addition, the crankshaft operates only in one direction, which is why automotive engines use a transmission. By multiplying the torque at low speeds, the transmission gets the car moving and allows the engine to operate at its optimum speed in the higher ranges.

Front-wheel drive vehicles such as the X-car use a combination transmission/differential, called a transaxle, instead of separate units connected by a driveshaft as in rear-wheel drive cars. The front drive axles are connected directly to the transaxle. This system is not only more compact, it's far more efficient than the conventional drivetrain. Because the transaxle contains fewer moving parts, less power-robbing friction is created. This means more of the power is delivered to the driving wheels.

Transaxles are either manual or automatic, just as with transmissions. (In this chapter, we'll discuss the 4-speed manual transaxle and cover the automatic version in a separate chapter.) The manual transaxle bolts directly to the transverse-mounted engine. All forward gears are in constant mesh, and synchronizers with blocker rings controlled by shift forks make gear selection and shifting easy. Reverse gear is obtained with a sliding idler gear arrangement.

The manual transaxle differs from a conventional manual transmission in several ways. The input gear, output gear, and differential are all supported by preloaded, tapered roller bearings. The correct preload is established by using selective shims under the right-hand bearing cups. Power is transmitted from the output shaft to the differential through a drive gear on the shaft which meshes with a ring or final drive gear bolted to the differential case.

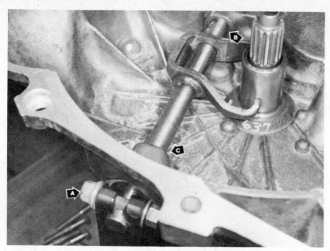

The clutch fork is welded to the shaft assembly. To replace it, remove bolt (A), rotate the shaft 90 degrees and withdraw it to free the end (B) from the case, and then lift the shaft up and remove it from (C).

The Clutch

If the engine is to idle without the car moving, a manual transaxle must be disconnected from the running engine. This is also necessary to permit starting the engine without rotating the transaxle gears and allow smooth shifts between the gears while the car is under way. A friction clutch located between the engine flywheel and the transaxle does this job.

The principal parts of any clutch mechanism are the driving members attached to the engine and rotating with it, the driven members attached to the transaxle and turning with it, and the operating members, which include the springs and linkage necessary to apply and release the pressure holding the driving and driven members in contact with each other.

The driving members include the rear surface of the engine flywheel and a pressure plate, a heavy flat ring with one side machined to a smooth surface. The driven members are the clutch disc itself, with linings of heat-resistant material (generally cotton and asbestos fibers woven or molded together). The linings are riveted to both surfaces of the driven plate. Fingers incorporated within the clutch are spring-loaded to squeeze the clutch disc between the flywheel and pressure plate. This provides a non-slip contact between the two. When depressed, the driver's clutch pedal causes the pressure plate to move away from the clutch disc. This allows the flywheel to rotate and the transaxle to either remain idle or to rotate at a different speed than the engine.

The clutch disc is the part most subject to wear in the clutch assembly. When badly worn, the flywheel and pressure plate can "slip" in relation to each other. You'll notice this problem when the engine tends to speed up under a load without the car's speed increasing. Replacing a clutch disc is a relatively simple matter once you have removed the transaxle from the car, but if allowed to wear badly, the rivets securing the lining to the disc can gouge or score the flywheel. If this happens, the flywheel will have to be removed and resurfaced at a machine shop. If the clutch on your X-car slips to the slightest degree when it's under a load, prepare to replace it soon.

Clutch Maintenance

There's not a great deal of maintenance/adjustment necessary with the X-car clutch. A self-adjusting quadrant assembly mounted to the clutch pedal is connected to the clutch fork lever by a fixed-length cable. This quadrant controls the cable tension and automatically makes any adjustments necessary whenever the pedal is depressed. This arrangement simplifies clutch operation and does away with the necessity of periodic adjustment.

You should, however, occasionally check the self-adjusting mechanism to be sure it's working. Locate the pawl above the quadrant and depress the clutch pedal. The pawl should engage firmly with the quadrant teeth. Now release the pedal and the bracket stop should lift the pawl away from the teeth.

A linkage operational check will determine if the clutch is releasing fully. Start the engine, place the transaxle in neutral, and set the parking brake. Depress and hold the clutch pedal at a point about ½ inch above the floor while you move the shift lever between first and reverse gears several times. You should be able to do this without clashing into reverse if the linkage is okay. If the shift is not smooth, the clutch is not releasing properly. Check the linkage for excess wear and/or damage.

To check the clutch fork travel, you'll need some-

The Neutral start switch is attached to the clutch pedal and prevents the engine from being started unless the transaxle is in Neutral or the clutch is depressed.

CLUTCH REPLACEMENT
If the clutch plate or release bearing fails, the transaxle assembly must be removed from the vehicle to permit clutch service. It is not recommended that transaxle removal be attempted by other than qualified servicemen with access to the necessary tools and proper equipment. Should any clutch service beyond normal maintenance and adjustment be necessary, it is strongly suggested you see your GM dealer.

Clutch and Manual Transaxle

one to sit in the driver's seat and hold the clutch pedal to the floor while you watch the clutch fork move at the transaxle. The end of the clutch fork lever should move between 1.6 and 1.8 inches.

Transaxle Maintenance

Like current manual transmissions, the transaxle is almost breakproof and should easily last the life of the car unless it is mistreated or is not properly maintained. An occasional fluid level check and shift cable adjustment are all that is required to keep the transaxle in good condition.

Unlike conventional manual transmissions, the X-car transaxle uses Dexron II automatic transmission fluid instead of hypoid gear oil. To check the fluid level, locate the filler plug on the outboard side of the transaxle case (see drawing) and remove it. Stick your little finger inside the hole; the fluid should be within ½ inch of the filler hole's lower edge. If it isn't, add sufficient fluid to bring it up to the correct level. The easiest way to do this is with a short-neck oil can filled with Dexron II. A few squeezes should do the trick. Replace the plug and tighten it snugly.

Under normal operating conditions, the manual transaxle fluid does not require draining and replacement, as does the automatic transaxle. When the level remains constantly low despite periodic topping up, you've got a leak. Check the axle shaft and shift lever seals; then, tighten the clutch cover. If the fluid level does not stabilize, one of the internal seals is leaking and the transaxle will have to be

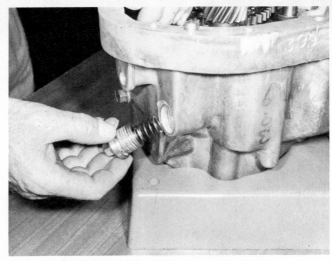

This is the reverse inhibitor fitting into which the transaxle shifter shaft fits. This fitting need not be removed to overhaul the transaxle.

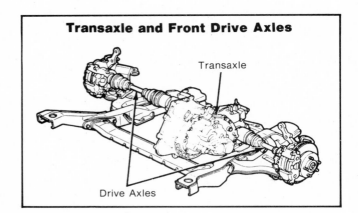

Transaxle and Front Drive Axles

Transaxle

Drive Axles

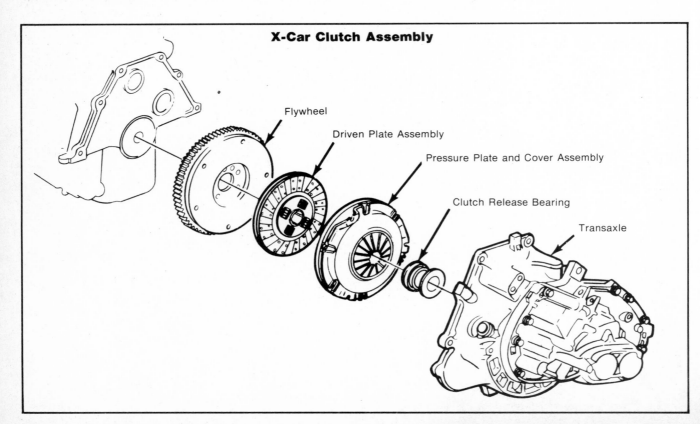

X-Car Clutch Assembly

Flywheel

Driven Plate Assembly

Pressure Plate and Cover Assembly

Clutch Release Bearing

Transaxle

The manual transaxle has an unusual lubrication path. Oil passes under the plastic oil scoop at two points. (The scoop has been moved out of the way to show oil travel path.) It passes through an internal case passage to the bearing cup bore.

removed and disassembled to stop the leak.

Two cables are used to move the shifter shaft—the transaxle select cable and the transaxle shift cable. Shift cable adjustment is made with the transaxle in first gear. To do so, remove the shift knob, boot, and retainer inside the driver's compartment. Fit a pair of 5/32-inch drill bits or pins in the alignment holes in the control assembly. This will hold the assembly in the first gear position. Now connect the two shift cables to the control assembly with the studs and pin retainers.

Push the transaxle rail selector shaft down until you feel a slight spring resistance. This places the transaxle in first gear. Rotate the shift lever counter-clockwise and install cable A (see page 102) to the shift lever slot. Install cable B to the other shift lever slot while pulling lightly on the select lever to remove any lash. Remove the two drill bits at the control assembly and road test the car, checking for a good neutral gate feel when you shift.

When Something Goes Wrong

If you've never had a car equipped with a manual transaxle before, you should realize that transaxle gears are not as quiet as those in a transmission. There are two types of normal operating noise (see Normal Transaxle Noises sidebar), but

Normal Transaxle Noises

There are two types of noise peculiar to transaxle operation: gear rattle and neutral rollover rattle. Gear rattle is a repetitive metallic sound heard when the car is lugging in gear. Its intensity will increase with transaxle operating temperature and engine torque, but decrease as the car picks up speed. You're more likely to hear gear rattle with current transaxles, as their gear ratios have been selected to deliver maximum fuel economy.

Neutral rollover rattle is similar to gear rattle, but only heard when the engine is idling with the transaxle in neutral and the clutch is engaged. Its intensity increases with transaxle operating temperature and engine torque loading caused by engine-driven accessories, such as the alternator and air conditioning compressor. If the idle speed is too low, the noise will change to a clattering sound similar to that of marbles rolling around loose inside the transaxle. The sound will disappear once the transaxle is put in gear.

Transaxle Removal

The transaxle is connected to the engine (by six bolts) and to a crossmember mount. The engine, clutch, and transaxle assembly is housed in a removable subframe or "cradle," which also contains the front suspension control arms. This type of drivetrain mounting is used to isolate the passenger compartment from road noise and engine vibration. At the same time, it complicates home servicing of the engine and transaxle.

Since the transaxle is designed to be removed from underneath the car, this cradle attachment must be loosened and "split" or swung apart. Moving the cradle in this way is necessary to provide sufficient room for transaxle removal. At the same time, the engine must be supported with a special fixture to hold it in place.

No attempt should be made to remove the transaxle unless the car is on a properly designed hoist and a satisfactory transaxle jack is available to support the transaxle during the removal procedure. Attempting home removal of the transaxle with the car on jack stands is not only impractical, but highly dangerous. GM specifies 26 separate and distinct removal steps for the manual transaxle, which should give you some idea of just how complicated the procedure is.

Manual Transaxle Filler Plug Location

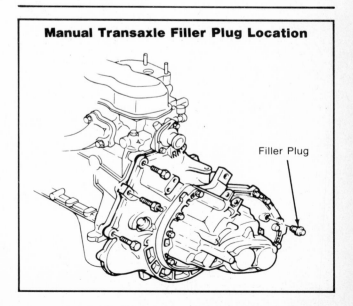

Filler Plug

Clutch and Manual Transaxle

most of the strange noises you'll hear are caused by the tires, wheel bearings, or exhaust system, rather than the transaxle.

A road test and a good ear are the most useful tools in determining what's causing a strange noise. Pick a smooth and level stretch of asphalt road and warm the car up to normal operating temperature. Accelerate, maintain a constant speed at light throttle, coast with the transaxle in gear, and let the engine run with the car stopped. Note the speed and gear at which the noise is heard; then compare what you heard to the following:

1. *Constant whining in one or more gears*—Transaxle gear noise, which may signal impending transaxle failure.
2. *Knocking or clicking on every other wheel rotation*—Rough wheel bearing, which may signal wheel bearing failure.
3. *Growling, grating, and/or vibration*—Can be an indication of three problems: bad bearings in transaxle, signal of possible transaxle failure; occurs even when car is coasting and transaxle is in neutral, signal of possible wheel bearing failure; if symptoms do not disappear when front wheels are raised off ground and engine is running with transaxle in gear, signal of possible differential bearing failure. (If noise does lessen or disappear, indicates wheel bearing problem.)

Preload Shim Selection

Whenever the input/output shaft or differential bearings are removed, the bearing cups must also be removed and the correct preload shim size re-established. This procedure requires using a special Chevy shim selector set (P/N J-26935), which contains three gauges, seven spacers and bolts, and a set of shims in various sizes. To select the proper preload shims:

1. With the input, output, and differential assemblies in the case, fit the three right-hand bearing cups on their respective bearings.
2. Position the gauges on the bearing cups. The cup should fit smoothly into each gauge bore.
3. Install the metal oil shield retainer into the bore on top of the output shaft gauge.
4. Place the clutch cover over the case and gauges. Position the spacers evenly around the case perimeter and install bolts.
5. Alternately tighten the spacer bolts to draw the cover to the case. Torque the bolts to 10 ft.-lbs. to compress the gauge sleeves.
6. Rotate each gauge to seat the bearing. Rotate the differential case three times in each direction.
7. Once the gauges are compressed, compare the gap between the outer sleeve and the base pad of each gauge to various shims. The correct shim size is the largest one you can draw through the gap without binding.
8. Select all three shims; then, remove the clutch cover, spacers, and gauges.
9. Put the shims in their proper bores in the clutch cover and add the metal shield; then, install the bearing cups. Special GM tools (P/N J-26936, J-23423-A, and J-26938) are recommended for bearing cup installation.

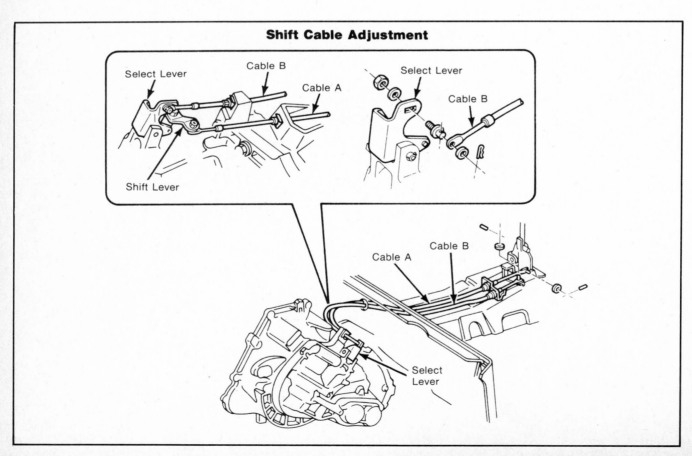

Shift Cable Adjustment

From the bearing cup bore, oil then passes through the output shaft and this nylon insert.

Oil from the output shaft travels under the nylon insert in the case bearing cup to the other bearing cup and back up through the input shaft.

Cradle Attachment

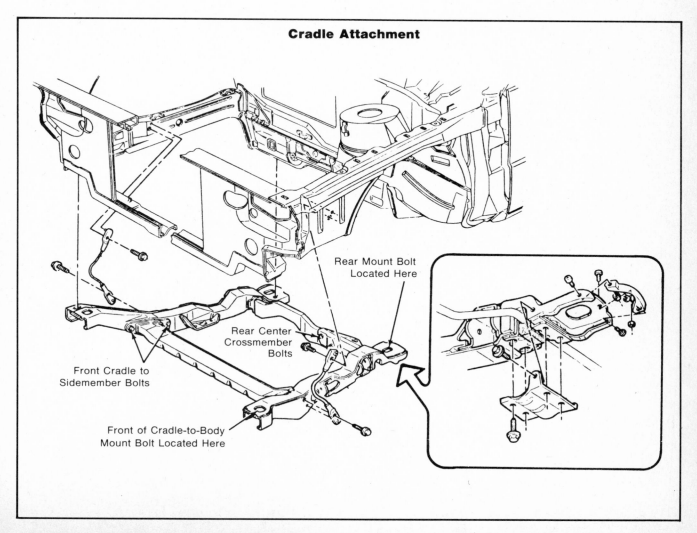

Rear Mount Bolt Located Here

Rear Center Crossmember Bolts

Front Cradle to Sidemember Bolts

Front of Cradle-to-Body Mount Bolt Located Here

Clutch and Manual Transaxle

Transaxle Overhaul

We've provided an exploded drawing of the manual transaxle for those who wish to tackle their own overhaul job. If this seems above and beyond your time, talent, or interest, you can at least gain a better understanding of how the transaxle works. And if you have to have it repaired, you'll know what the shop is doing.

For those who want to do it at home, an overhaul sequence is presented in pictorial how-to format. Remember, however, that the transaxle used for our sequence may not be exactly like yours. General Motors, like other automotive manufacturers, continually makes running changes during each model year to improve driveability and durability of major components such as transaxles. If for any reason you find a deviation between our sequence and your transaxle, seek the advice of a qualified transaxle shop—don't guess about what you're doing.

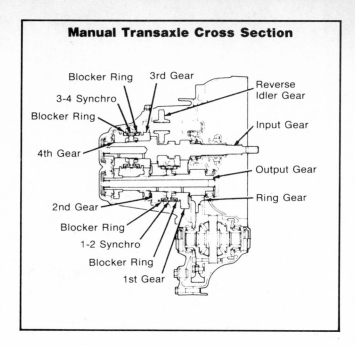

Manual Transaxle Cross Section

Manual Transaxle Components

1. CASE ASSEMBLY
2. VENT ASSEMBLY
3. MAGNET
4. PIN
5. WASHER, Drain Screw
6. SCREW, Drain
7. BOLT
8. WASHER, Fill Plug
9. PLUG, Fill
10. SEAL ASSEMBLY, Axle Shaft
11. PLUG
12. SHIELD, Oil
13. BEARING ASSEMBLY
14. GEAR, 4th Speed Output
15. RING, 3rd Speed Output Gear Retaining
16. GEAR, 3rd Speed Output
17. GEAR, 2nd Speed Output
18. RING, Synchronizer Blocking
19. RING, Synchronizer Retaining
20. SPRING, Synchronizer Key Retaining
21. KEY, Synchronizer
22. SYNCHRONIZER ASSEMBLY
23. GEAR, 1st Speed Output
24. SLEEVE, Oil Shield
25. GEAR, Output
26. BEARING ASSEMBLY, Output
27. SHIM, Output Gear Bearing Adjustment
28. SHIELD, Output Bearing Oil
29. RETAINER, Output Gear Bearing Oil Shield
30. GEAR, 4th Speed Input
31. SYNCHRONIZER ASSEMBLY
32. GEAR, 3rd Speed Input
33. GEAR, Input Cluster
34. BEARING ASSEMBLY, Input
35. SCREW
36. SHIM, Input Gear Bearing Adjustment
37. SEAL ASSEMBLY, Input Gear
38. RETAINER, Input Gear
39. RETAINER ASSEMBLY, Input Gear Bearing
40. SEAL, Input Gear Bearing Retainer
41. BEARING ASSEMBLY, Clutch Release
42. SCREW & WASHER, Reverse Idler
43. SHAFT, Reverse Idler
44. GEAR ASSEMBLY, Reverse Idler
45. SPACER, Reverse Idler Shaft
46. HOUSING ASSEMBLY, Clutch & Differential
47. SCREW
48. RETAINER, Speedo Gear Fitting
49. SLEEVE, Speedo Driven Gear
50. SEAL, Speedo Gear Sleeve
51. GEAR, Speedo Driven
52. SEAT, Reverse Inhibitor Spring
53. SPRING, Reverse Inhibitor
54. PIN
55. LEVER, Reverse Shift
56. STUD, Reverse Lever Locating
57. LEVER ASSEMBLY, Detent
58. WASHER, Lock Detent Lever
59. SPRING, Detent
60. BOLT
61. SHAFT, Shift
62. SEAL ASSEMBLY, Shift Shaft
63. BOLT
64. NUT
65. INTERLOCK, Shift
66. SHIM, Shift Shaft
67. WASHER, Reverse Inhibitor Spring
68. FORK, 3rd & 4th Shift
69. SHAFT, Shift Fork
70. SCREW
71. GUIDE, Oil
72. FORK, 1st & 2nd Shift
73. SEAL ASSEMBLY, Clutch Fork Shaft
74. BEARING, Clutch Fork Shaft
75. SHAFT ASSEMBLY, Clutch Fork
76. DIFFERENTIAL ASSEMBLY
77. BEARING ASSEMBLY, Differential
78. CASE, Differential
79. SHAFT, Differential Pinion
80. GEAR, Speedo Drive
81. SHIM, Differential Bearing Adjustment
82. WASHER, Pinion Thrust
83. GEAR, Differential Pinion
84. WASHER, Side Gear Thrust
85. GEAR, Differential Side
86. LOCKWASHER
87. SCREW, Pinion shaft
88. GEAR, Differential Ring
89. BOLT

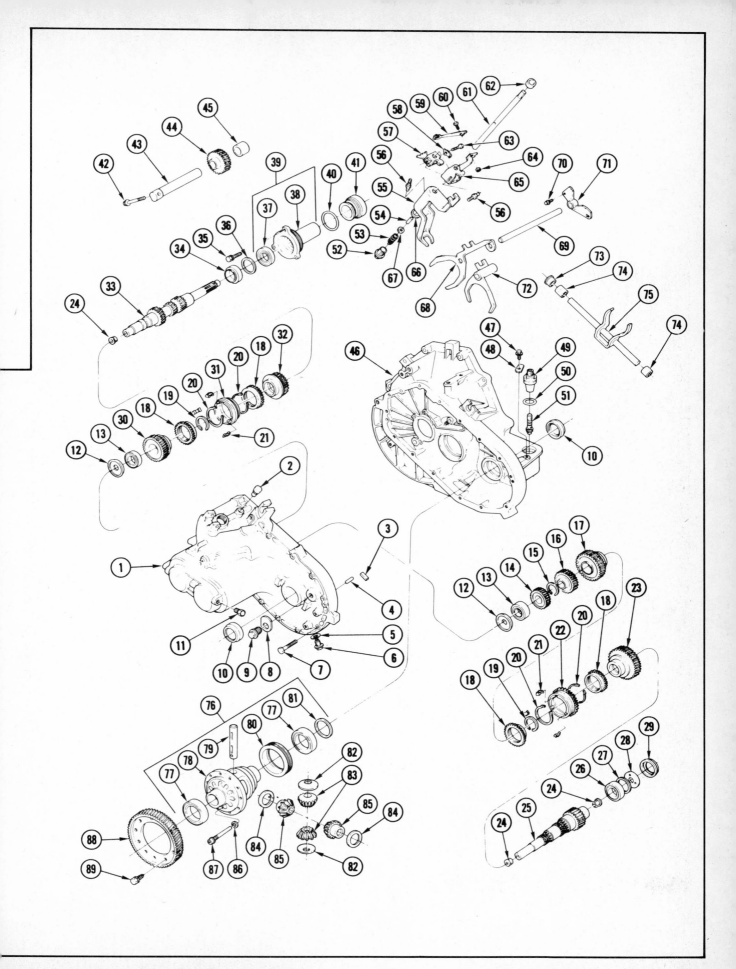

1. To overhaul the manual transaxle, place it on a suitable workbench area or in the special workstand (P/N J-28408) recommended by GM and remove the clutch throwout bearing.

2. Turn the transaxle over on its clutch housing and loosen the 15 bolts that hold the clutch cover to the transaxle case; then return the unit to its original position for bolt removal.

3. The bolts are removed in this manner. If the clutch cover and case are separated, with the clutch cover facing down, you'll have a real mess on your hands.

4. This is the correct way to split the clutch cover/transaxle case. Anaerobic sealant is used instead of a gasket, so you may have to break the cover free by tapping.

5. Grasp the ring gear/differential assembly as shown and lift it out of the case. Side gears can be replaced by removing the pinion shaft (arrow); the rest of the assembly is serviced as a unit.

6. Turn the shifter shaft to position the gears in neutral. Bend back the lock tab on the lock and remove this bolt from the shifter shaft assembly to free the shaft for removal.

7. The shifter shaft can now be withdrawn from the transaxle case as shown. It is not necessary to remove the reverse inhibitor plug from the opposite side of the case for shaft removal.

8. Lift the shift fork shaft up and remove it from the case. It may be necessary to wiggle the shaft as you pull upward in order to free it from the shift forks.

9. Disengage the reverse shift fork from the guide pin in the case and interlock bracket. Remove the fork from transaxle case. Again, it may be necessary to work it free.

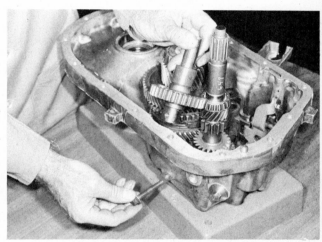

10. Loosen and remove the lock bolt from outside the case which holds the reverse idler gear shaft in place. Remove gear/shaft/spacer assembly as shown.

11. Remove the detent shift lever and interlock assembly from the transaxle case. Leave the shift forks engaged with synchronizers on input and output shafts.

12. Grasp the input and output shafts as shown and remove them from the case as an assembly with the shift forks intact. This is a heavy handful.

13. Note the shift forks' position for reassembly and remove the 3rd-4th fork from the shaft assembly. This was a weak point of early transaxles, so inspect the fork carefully.

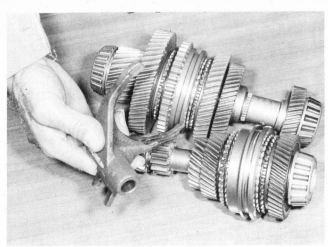

14. Remove the 1st-2nd shift fork and inspect it for wear or damage. Input and output gear trains require a hydraulic press for disassembly.

15. If the bearing cup must be removed from the clutch cover or transaxle case, a special bearing cup remover (P/N J-26941) must be used with a slide hammer.

16. Here is the removed output shaft right-hand bearing cup. To remove the input shaft right-hand bearing cup, the retainer (arrow) must be unbolted and removed for access to bearing cup.

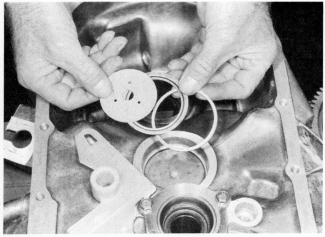

17. Remove the external oil ring, internal oil seal, and selective shim from the bearing cup bore. The shim size must be checked whenever the bearing cup is replaced or the shaft gear train disassembled.

18. To begin the input shaft gear train disassembly, carefully pry the nylon oil seal from the input shaft base. The output shaft contains a similar oil seal.

19. A universal bearing remover can be used instead of the various special removers recommended. Fit the remover under the input shaft 4th gear as shown and tighten in place.

20. To prevent damage to the input shaft and/or bearing, insert this pilot (P/N J-26943) into the shaft. Then press off the bearing and gear. This directs pressure against the shaft end instead of the bearing race.

21. Once the input shaft bearing and 4th gear are pressed free, inspect for wear/damage and place them on the workbench in the order removed from shaft.

22. Remove the brass blocker ring. Inspect the ring teeth for wear or damage and proceed with gear train disassembly. Do not disassemble the synchronizer unless necessary.

23. The snap ring must be removed from the shaft groove before the rest of the 3rd-4th synchronizer can be removed from the input shaft. Always install new snap rings upon reassembly.

24. The 3rd-4th synchronizer can be removed without a press. Simply push the assembly off the input shaft. Check the synchronizer carefully and set to one side.

25. Third gear may slide off the shaft. If it does not, use support plates and press the gear from the input shaft. Inspect the gear teeth for signs of wear or damage.

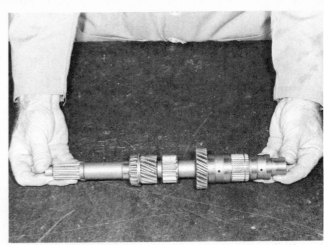

26. The right-hand bearing remains on the input shaft, but it can be pressed off if desired. The cluster gear arrangement is an integral part of the shaft, and should be inspected carefully.

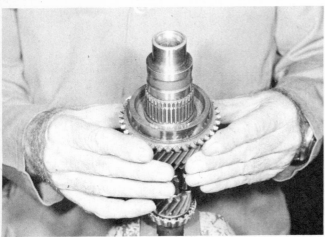

27. To begin input shaft reassembly, fit 3rd gear on the input shaft and seat it against the cluster gear. The gear may have to be pressed in place on shaft.

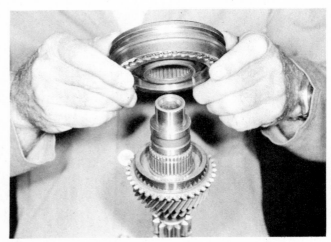

28. Fit the brass blocker ring to the underside of 3rd-4th synchronizer assembly and install it on the input shaft, rotating assembly to mesh with 3rd gear.

29. Install a new snap ring on the input shaft and make sure it fits properly into the snap ring groove. Snap ring installation is an easy step to overlook.

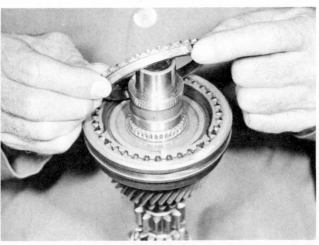

30. Reinstall the second brass blocker ring on the synchronizer once the snap ring has been replaced. Rotate the blocker ring to engage synchronizer assembly.

31. Place the input shaft in a press with 4th gear and left-hand bearing positioned as shown; then install pilot (P/N J-26943) and press the bearing and gear on shaft.

32. To disassemble the output shaft, use support plates and pilot. Repeat the procedure used with input shaft. Inspect bearing and 4th gear for wear or damage.

33. Remove the snap ring from the output shaft. This holds 3rd gear in place. The output gear train disassembly is essentially a repeat of the input gear train disassembly procedure.

34. Use support plates and pilot to press both 3rd and 2nd speed gears from the output shaft. Be sure to hold onto the shaft under the press when removing the gears.

35. Remove the brass blocker ring from the 1st-2nd synchronizer and spread the snap ring which holds the 1st-2nd synchronizer in place. Remove the snap ring from output shaft.

36. Remove 1st-2nd synchronizer and 1st speed gear from the output shaft. In some cases, you may have to press 1st gear from the output shaft.

37. *The right-hand bearing is shown here on the output shaft, but it can be pressed off if necessary. Inspect the shaft carefully for worn or damaged teeth before reassembly.*

38. *Install 1st speed gear on the output shaft, using the press if necessary to seat it completely; then install 1st-2nd synchronizer assembly with brass blocker ring.*

39. *This snap ring must be installed to hold 1st-2nd synchronizer in place before further gear train buildup can be accomplished. Seat the snap ring properly in the shaft groove.*

40. *Replace other blocker ring on assembled 1st-2nd synchronizer. Note how the tang on the blocker ring fits into the groove in the synchronizer for easy installation.*

41. *Continue output shaft gear train buildup by installing 2nd speed gear; then install 3rd speed gear as shown. Gears should drop in place on the shaft splines.*

42. *Install the snap ring to hold 3rd speed gear in place. Use new snap rings for reassembly and seat them completely in the shaft groove before proceeding with 4th gear installation.*

43. Position 4th speed gear and left-hand bearing on the output shaft. Bearing and gear must both be pressed back onto the output shaft with proper tools.

44. Fit the output shaft assembly in the press as shown. Install a pilot in the shaft end and press 4th gear and left-hand bearing on the output shaft until fully seated.

45. With the input and output shafts both reassembled, position them as shown and install both shift forks in their respective synchronizers.

46. Grasp the input and output shafts as shown with shift forks attached and lower them into the transaxle case, seating the shaft bearings in the appropriate bearing cups.

47. Place the ring gear/differential assembly in the transaxle case to mesh with the output shaft as shown. Rotate ring gear to check mesh with output shaft gear.

48. A shim selector set (P/N J-26935) is required to establish the proper preload shim selection. Fit the clutch cover bearing cups over the shaft bearings and install gauges as shown.

49. Replace the clutch cover and install the shim selector spacers evenly around case perimeter. See the text for proper procedure in selecting shims.

50. After the preload shim selection is made, reinstall the bearing cups in the clutch cover using a slide hammer and bearing installer tool—do not try to install with an ordinary hammer.

51. Position the interlock bracket on the guide pin so that the bracket engages the shift fork fingers. Place the detent shift lever into the interlock bracket mechanism.

52. Install the reverse idler gear and shaft with the large chamfered ends of the gear teeth facing up. The flat on the shaft must face the input gear shaft when correctly installed.

53. Replace the spacer on the reverse idler gear shaft, check gear mesh with input gear; then install the lock bolt from outside of case. Torque bolt to 16 ft.-lbs.

54. Install the reverse shift fork on the guide pin, making sure the shift fork engages the interlock bracket properly. This sets up the case for shifter shaft installation.

55. Install the shift fork shaft through the synchronizer forks and seat shaft into the case bore. You may have to wiggle the shaft into place to seat it completely.

56. Insert the shifter shaft through the case and reverse shift fork using a rotary motion until it fits into the reverse inhibitor spring spacer.

57. Align the shifter shaft in neutral position and install the lock bolt through the detent shift lever. Tighten the bolt in place and bend the lock tab over the bolt head.

58. Check the shift fork operation by working the shifter shaft through each gear position. Shifts should be smooth, with no binding or clashing of gears.

59. Run a thin bead of anaerobic sealant along the clutch cover flange; then install the cover using dowel pins at each end of the case as guides.

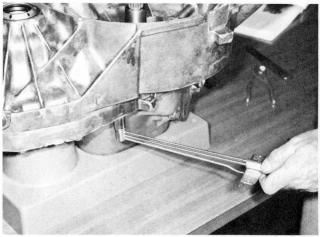

60. Install the case-to-cover bolts and alternately tighten to draw the cover down evenly. Torque these bolts to 16 ft.-lbs. and recheck the shift operation through all gears.

11

125 Automatic Transaxle

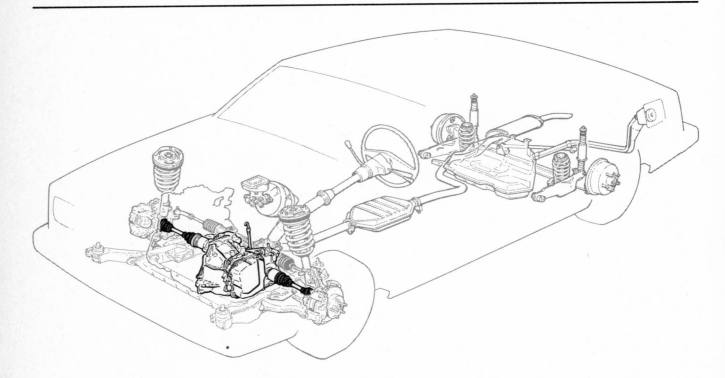

X-cars without a manual transaxle use the 125 automatic transaxle. This unit contains the same major components as any conventional automatic transmission—a torque converter, compound planetary gear set, three multiple-disc clutches, a roller clutch, and a servo-operated band. Operation of these transaxle components is pretty much the same as with an automatic transmission, but the design and terminology differ somewhat. Here's how the 125 automatic transaxle differs from a typical Turbo Hydra-matic transmission.

The torque converter is located to the side of the main transaxle body, instead of directly in front of it, and two sprockets and a chain drive transmit engine torque to the output shaft and differential. This design gives the 125 an odd L-shaped appearance. When the unit is bolted to the engine, its main body rests to the rear. As a result of the L-shaped design,

the oil sump is very shallow and insufficient to do its job. To assure proper fluid circulation, the valve body cover is used as a second oil sump. A thermostatic valve lets the transaxle fluid move between the two sumps according to transaxle temperature.

When the transaxle temperature exceeds 125 degrees F, fluid is pumped into the valve cover. This prevents foaming in the lower part of the transaxle. The oil pan fluid then drops from its cold level. Once the transaxle cools, the thermostatic valve opens and fluid flows back from the valve cover to the oil pan, raising its level. This has an important bearing on checking the automatic transaxle fluid level, as we'll see, since the fluid level is *higher* when cold than when hot.

Due to the unique positioning of the torque converter above the main body, engine torque is routed through two 90-degree turns to reach the transaxle input shaft. From that point, it's a straight line to the

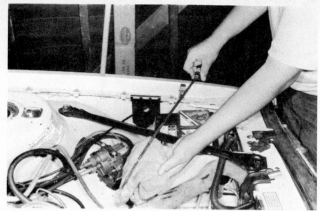

The ATF is checked by removing the transaxle dipstick with the engine idling at normal operating temperature and noting the indicated level. Note the color and condition of fluid on dipstick, too.

differential, which operates as a conventional differential by varying the speed of one drive axle relative to the other when the car goes around a corner.

Checking and Changing Fluid

Many drivers change their crankcase oil and oil filter faithfully, but totally ignore the same requirement for their automatic transaxle until a breakdown occurs. Just as heat causes engine oil to lose its effectiveness, the heat created inside a transaxle causes the automatic transmission fluid, or ATF, to wear out.

Unlike engine oil, excessive heat will cause the ATF to "burn," destroying its lubricating qualities quickly and changing its characteristic reddish color to a dark brown or black. This in turn takes its toll in clutch/band wear and eventually results in an expensive overhaul.

You should check your transmission fluid level at least as often as you check the crankcase oil level. The basic difference in procedure is simply that while the crankcase oil is checked when the engine is cold, ATF level should be checked with the engine at normal operating temperature and idling.

To check the ATF level correctly, the vehicle should be on a level surface, with the engine operating at normal temperature and the transaxle selector lever placed in Park. Remove the dipstick and wipe it clean, then reinsert it fully in the filler tube and remove a second time. Hold the dipstick horizontally and note where the fluid level ends. Because of the shape of the filler tube, the fluid level may be a little misleading, so look carefully for a full oil ring on both sides of the dipstick.

When the fluid is at normal operating temperature, it should be to the "Full Hot" mark or in the hatched area of the dipstick. Since it only takes one pint of fluid to bring the level from the "Add" to the "Full" mark, ATF should be added in small quantities to avoid overfilling. Like too much engine oil, too much ATF will eventually cause damage.

If necessary, it's possible to check the transaxle fluid level when cold. Look at the dipstick above the hatched area and you'll see two tiny dimples. When the transaxle is cold, the fluid should be between

Transaxle Removal

The transaxle is connected to the engine and to a crossmember mount. The engine, converter, and transaxle assembly are housed in a removable subframe or "cradle" assembly which also contains the front suspension control arms. This type of drivetrain mounting is used to isolate the passenger compartment from road noise and engine vibration. At the same time, it complicates home servicing of the engine and transaxle.

Since the transaxle is designed to be removed from underneath the car, this cradle attachment must be loosened and "split" or swung apart. Moving the cradle in this way is necessary to provide sufficient room for transaxle removal. At the same time, the engine must be supported with a special fixture to hold it in place.

No attempt should be made to remove the transaxle unless the car is on a properly designed hoist and a satisfactory transaxle jack is available to support the transaxle during the removal procedure. Attempting home removal of the transaxle with the car on jackstands is not only impractical, but highly dangerous as it can lead to serious injury. GM specifies 32 separate and distinct removal steps for the automatic transaxle, which should give you some idea of just how complicated the procedure can be.

these two dimples. If it isn't, you need fluid, but it's a good idea to wait and add it when the transaxle is at normal operating temperature, as overfilling is an even greater possibility when the fluid is cold.

When checking the ATF level, also note its condition. Wipe the dipstick on a clean white cloth or paper towel. ATF contains a reddish dye that helps you distinguish it from crankcase oil or power steering fluid. This is helpful when you're trying to determine what those spots are underneath your car and where they're coming from, a problem we'll get to shortly.

If the stain on the cloth or paper towel is brownish or black, it tells you that the fluid has "burned" and that something is wrong inside the transaxle. Changing fluid at this point will not help—what you need now is an overhaul. The idea behind transaxle care and maintenance is to prevent this from happening. One of the best ways to do so is to change the fluid and filter at periodic intervals.

GM recommends that you change the transaxle fluid and replace the strainer every 100,000 miles, unless you drive under conditions considered to be

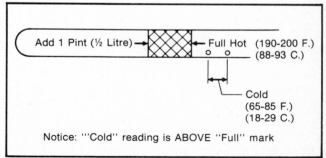

Keep the transaxle oil level within the hatch-marked area on the dipstick.

125 Automatic Transaxle

"severe," such as heavy city traffic, in hilly or mountainous areas, or during very warm weather. We'd suggest you change the fluid and strainer every 15,000 miles, regardless. With today's high underhood and engine operating temperatures, it's easy enough for transaxle fluid temperatures to soar over 250 degrees F, and even more if you're towing, driving in the desert, or climbing long hills. By changing the ATF periodically, you're replacing it before it has a chance to break down and lose its lubricating and heat-absorbing qualities. The extra cost is not great when you compare it to the smoother operation and longer life of your transaxle. Four quarts of Dexron II will do the job.

The TV control cable (A) connects the carburetor throttle valve to the transaxle. The shift cable (B) selects the proper drive range.

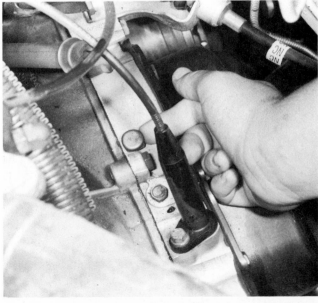

The Oil Cooler

Like engine coolant, transaxle fluid absorbs heat during normal operation. To get rid of the heat and cool the fluid, it travels through a metal line to an oil cooler located in the side tank of the radiator. This sealed container inside the radiator tank absorbs the heat and sends the cooled fluid back to the transaxle through a return line. If the transaxle develops a major problem internally, the oil cooler should be flushed with solvent to remove any metal particles.

Fluid Leaks

Due to the compact packaging within the X-car engine compartment, fluid leaks can be deceiving. If you find a small puddle of fluid or oil on the garage floor or on the driveway, it's a sure sign that something's wrong. Before jumping to any conclusion, first determine what kind of fluid is leaking. Reference to the troubleshooting chart in the Driveway Service chapter will help you here—engine oil is brown, transaxle fluid is red, power steering fluid is green or blue, and engine coolant is

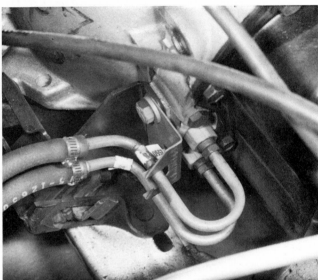

Possible transaxle fluid leakage points include the filler pipe seal at the transaxle (A), the oil cooler connections (B), and the transaxle vent (C).

125 Automatic Transaxle Cross Section

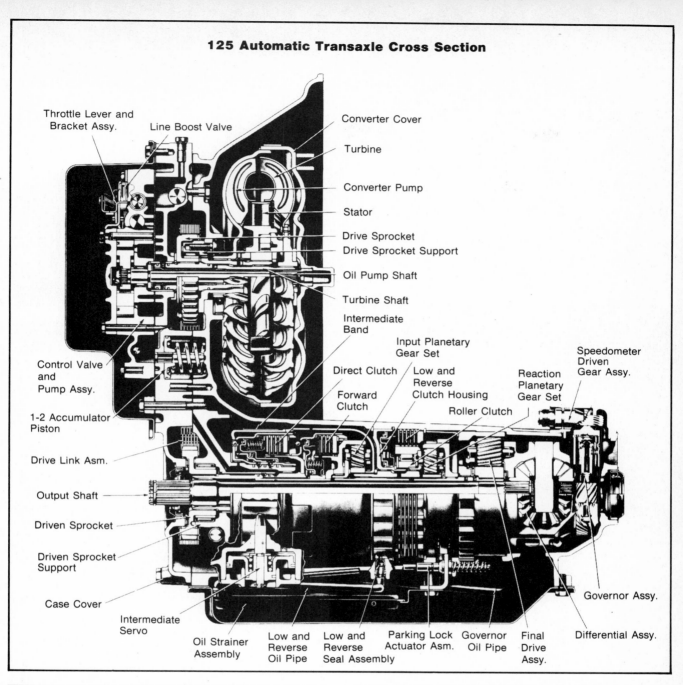

Throttle Lever and Bracket Assy.

Line Boost Valve

Converter Cover

Turbine

Converter Pump

Stator

Drive Sprocket

Drive Sprocket Support

Oil Pump Shaft

Turbine Shaft

Intermediate Band

Input Planetary Gear Set

Direct Clutch

Low and Reverse Clutch Housing

Forward Clutch

Reaction Planetary Gear Set

Speedometer Driven Gear Assy.

Roller Clutch

Control Valve and Pump Assy.

1-2 Accumulator Piston

Drive Link Asm.

Output Shaft

Driven Sprocket

Driven Sprocket Support

Case Cover

Intermediate Servo

Oil Strainer Assembly

Low and Reverse Oil Pipe

Low and Reverse Seal Assembly

Parking Lock Actuator Asm.

Governor Oil Pipe

Final Drive Assy.

Governor Assy.

Differential Assy.

Transaxle Torque Converter

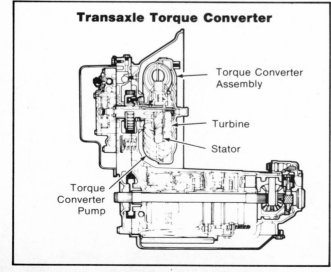

Torque Converter Assembly

Turbine

Stator

Torque Converter Pump

Chain Drive

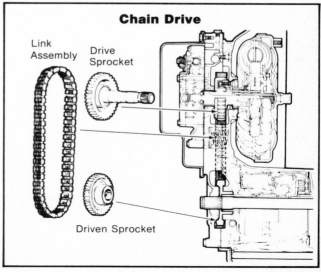

Link Assembly

Drive Sprocket

Driven Sprocket

green in color.

When a leak of any kind develops around the engine and transaxle, the fluid is usually carried to the rear by the air stream passing underneath the vehicle. This makes exact leak location difficult. To trace it down when you can't see exactly where the leak is coming from, clean the suspected area with solvent to remove all of the fluid stains. Start the engine, drive the car around the block a few times and then check the following areas:

1. Transaxle pan or valve body cover
2. Filler pipe seal
3. Throttle valve cable seal
4. Speedometer driven gear O-ring
5. Oil cooler connector fittings
6. Converter seal (remove shield)

A leak at any of these points can be taken care of without removing the transaxle from the car. Other points of leakage, such as the manual valve bore plug or line pressure pickup pipe plug, require transaxle removal and/or partial transaxle disassembly.

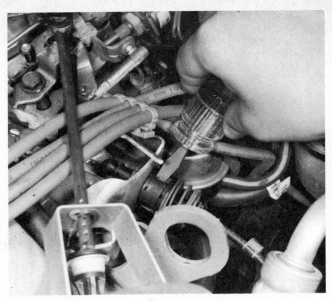

To adjust the TV control cable, depress and hold the lock tab, pull the slider back until it stops, and then release the lock tab.

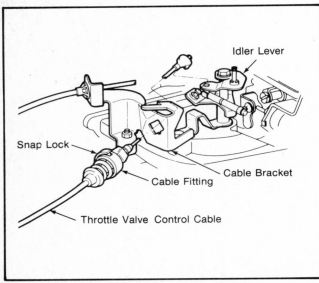

The TV control cable connection at the carburetor

TV Control Cable Adjustment

Most shift problems are caused either by a low fluid level or incorrect adjustment of the throttle valve (TV) control cable. Throttle pressure controls the shift points of the transaxle according to engine load. The 125 throttle valve is operated by a cable connected to the carburetor throttle linkage. When you depress the accelerator pedal, the carburetor throttle plates open and the cable relays the movement to the throttle valve inside the transaxle.

Whenever the carburetor idle speed is changed, the TV cable adjustment should be checked. If the carburetor is removed or the transaxle pulled for

overhaul, the cable should also be readjusted in the following manner:

1. Locate the snap lock on the TV cable fitting. It's bracket-mounted on the engine near the carburetor.
2. Make sure that the cable will slide through the snap lock without binding.
3. Check to see that the cable sealing tube is securely mounted to the transaxle case.
4. Open the carburetor idler lever to its full or wide open throttle position. The idler lever must touch the idler lever stop.
5. Now push the snap lock fitting down into the hole in the cable fitting bracket until the top of the lock is flush with the rest of the fitting.
6. Release the snap lock and the adjustment is completed.

Gear Selector Cable

If the gear selector cable is replaced, it must also be adjusted. Place the shift lever in Neutral and disconnect the cable from its lever at the transaxle. Move the cable lever clockwise to the first or Low detent, then counterclockwise through four detents to Neutral. Reconnect the cable to the lever with the attaching pin, and tighten the pin nut carefully to keep the lever from slipping into the Park position. Move the shift lever through the range and check the instrument panel shift indicator movement—it should coincide with the cable detent positions.

Overhauling the 125

Removal, teardown, overhaul, and reassembly of the 125 automatic transaxle is a step beyond the manual transaxle and the amateur mechanic. If you don't have a good set of tools, a clean place in which to work, and a better-than-average understanding of an automatic transaxle, our

Forward Clutch Assembly

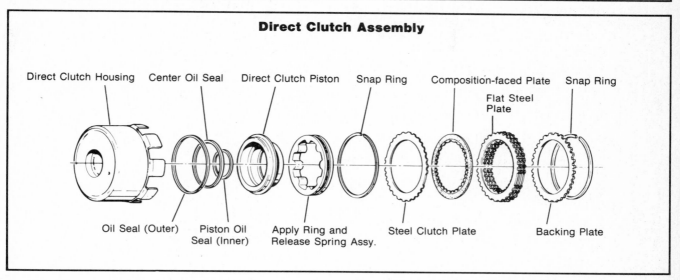

Selective Snap Ring · Forward Clutch Housing · Piston Oil Seal (Inner) · Apply Ring · Release Spring · Waved Steel Plate · Flat Steel Plate · Snap Ring

Oil Seal Rings · Piston Oil Seal (Outer) · Forward Clutch Piston · Release Spring Guide · Snap Ring · Composition-faced Plate · Backing Plate

Direct Clutch Assembly

Direct Clutch Housing · Center Oil Seal · Direct Clutch Piston · Snap Ring · Composition-faced Plate · Flat Steel Plate · Snap Ring

Oil Seal (Outer) · Piston Oil Seal (Inner) · Apply Ring and Release Spring Assy. · Steel Clutch Plate · Backing Plate

Reaction Gear Set

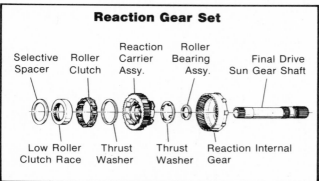

Selective Spacer · Roller Clutch · Reaction Carrier Assy. · Roller Bearing Assy. · Final Drive Sun Gear Shaft

Low Roller Clutch Race · Thrust Washer · Thrust Washer · Reaction Internal Gear

Low/Reverse Clutch

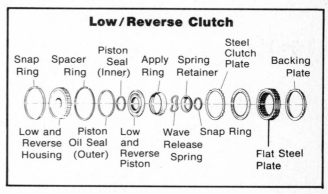

Snap Ring · Spacer Ring · Piston Seal (Inner) · Apply Ring · Spring Retainer · Steel Clutch Plate · Backing Plate

Low and Reverse Housing · Piston Oil Seal (Outer) · Low and Reverse Piston · Wave Release Spring · Snap Ring · Flat Steel Plate

Input Unit

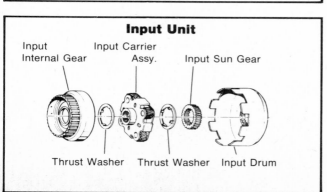

Input Internal Gear · Input Carrier Assy. · Input Sun Gear

Thrust Washer · Thrust Washer · Input Drum

Intermediate Servo

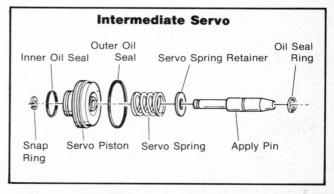

Inner Oil Seal · Outer Oil Seal · Servo Spring Retainer · Oil Seal Ring

Snap Ring · Servo Piston · Servo Spring · Apply Pin

125 Automatic Transaxle

best advice is: *don't try it.* Aside from patience, attention to instructions, and the use of the proper tools (many of which are special GM tools for use with the 125), cleanliness is most important. Automatics won't tolerate dirt inside for very long. Use clean solvent on all components as you remove them from the case. If they are not to be given any further attention until reassembly, lubricate them with ATF (nothing else) and store them in plastic bags to keep them clean.

If you decide to tackle the 125 yourself, you'll need a number of special tools in addition to the usual assortment of wrenches and other basic tools.

When installing a new TV control cable, connect it to the throttle idler lever (arrow) and rotate the lever to its full-travel stop position. This sets the automatic cable adjuster correctly when the throttle idler lever is released.

As you follow the pictorial disassembly sequence, you'll find frequent references to "inspect for wear or damage." Those who are knowledgeable in transmission/transaxle overhaul procedures will know what to look for—beginners may wonder exactly what constitutes "wear and damage." A list of common defects is provided below to guide you in the inspection procedure:

Band—burning, flaking, or missing lining
Case—cracks or porosity (ATF leaks through metal)
Bushings—scoring or cracking
Clutch piston/Apply ring—distortion or cracks
Clutch spring/Retainer assembly—broken, distorted, or cracked springs; bent retainer
Link assembly—loose links
Piston feed holes—plugging
Clutch plates—friction surface burned, worn, or missing
Sprocket/gear teeth/splines—cracks, nicks, burrs, or scoring
Snap ring/Oil seal ring grooves—burrs
Thrust washers—scoring, pitting, distortion, or rough surface
(If needle-bearing type, check to make sure all bearings are intact and operate smoothly.)

The shift cable adjustment (described in text) is made at the circled area.

Transaxle I.D.

While the basic 125 automatic transaxle design is the same regardless of whether it is used in a Citation, Omega, Phoenix, or Skylark, there may be internal individual variations according to model year and engine application. For this reason, the transaxle model code number is essential in obtaining the correct replacement parts. The model code location is shown below.

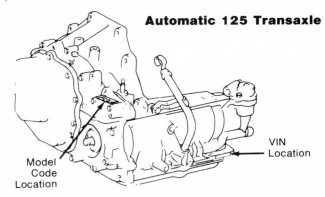

Automatic 125 Transaxle

VIN Location

Model Code Location

Since GM may revise the internal components and operation of their powertrains on a running basis, the procedures which are depicted in the following overhaul sequence, as well as the specifications, should be regarded as being representative of the correct overhaul procedure and specifications to follow. The transaxle used in the pictorial overhaul sequence is an early production model fitted to a 4-cylinder Phoenix and may not be exactly identical with later production models fitted to other X-cars. When overhauling your automatic transaxle, do not hesitate to check with your GM dealer should you encounter differences from those shown in our pictorial how-to sequence.

Differential/Final Drive

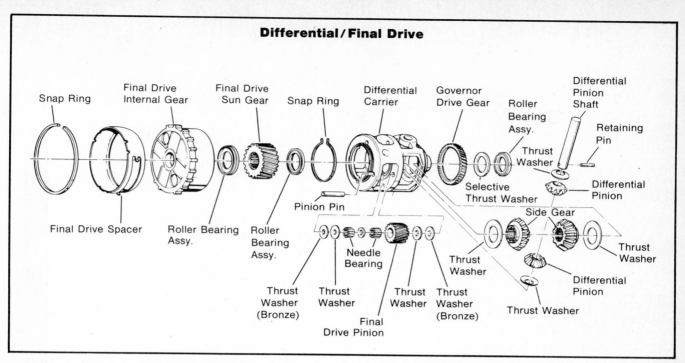

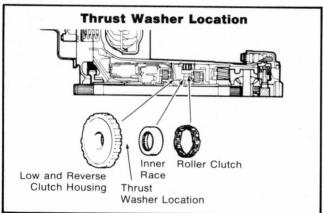

Thrust Washer Location

Low and Reverse Clutch Housing — Thrust Washer Location — Inner Race — Roller Clutch

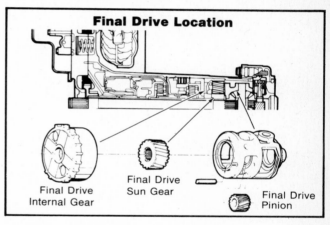

Final Drive Location

Final Drive Internal Gear — Final Drive Sun Gear — Final Drive Pinion

Models	Forward Clutch				
PZ, CV	Waved Plate No. / Thickness	Flat Steel Plate No. / Thickness	Comp. Faced Plate No.	Apply Ring I.D.* / Width	
	1 1.6 mm (0.06")	3 1.9 mm (0.08")	4	0 12 mm (0.47")	

125 Clutch Plate And Apply Ring Usage

Models	Direct Clutch			Low And Reverse Clutch		
PZ, CV	Flat Steel Plate No. / Thickness	Comp. Faced Plate No.	Apply Ring I.D.* / Width	Flat Steel No.	Comp. Faced Plate No.	Apply Ring I.D.* / Width
	4 2.3 mm (0.09")	4	7 19 mm (0.75")	5	5	0 15.4 mm (0.612")

The direct and forward clutch flat steel plates and the forward clutch waved steel plate should be identified by their thickness.

The direct and forward production-installed, composition-faced clutch plates must not be interchanged. For service, direct and forward clutch use the same composition-faced plates.

*Measure the width of the clutch apply ring for positive identification.

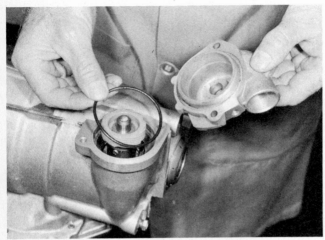

1. To overhaul the 125 automatic, place the transaxle in a holding fixture if available and remove the converter. Unbolt the governor cover and discard the O-ring seal.

2. Remove the governor cover-to-speedometer drive gear thrust washer and lift the governor/drive gear assembly from the transaxle case.

3. Rotate the transaxle in the holding fixture to position the oil pan up. Unbolt the oil pan with a 13mm socket and remove the pan from the case. Discard the old pan gasket.

4. Swivel the oil strainer to unhook it from the dipstick stop, then pull up on the opposite end to free the strainer assembly from the transaxle case. The strainer should not be reused.

5. The plastic/metal oil strainer assembly uses an O-ring seal on the nipple. If the seal does not come off with the strainer, retrieve it from the bore and discard.

6. Unbolt the retaining brackets (circled) and remove the low-reverse oil pipe by pulling it from the case. Retrieve the O-ring seal and backup ring from the bore (arrow).

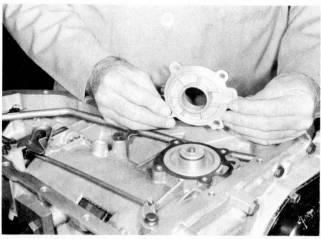

7. Unbolt the intermediate servo cover (the retaining bracket is held by one cover bolt) and remove it from the case. Peel the old gasket from the servo bore flange and discard.

8. Remove the intermediate servo assembly from the case. The oil seal rings should be replaced with a new set. The band apply pin requires a special tool to check.

9. Remove the third accumulator check valve. Early production models like this one use a cup plug to hold the valve in place and require the use of a No. 6 Easyout for removal.

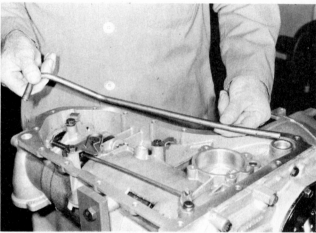

10. Remove the remaining oil pipe by pulling the curved end out of the case and rotating the pipe as you pull the straight end free from the case. Do not bend the pipes out of shape.

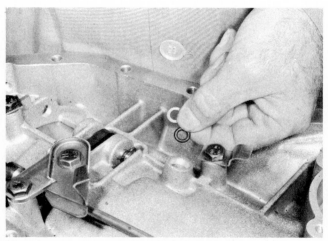

11. Low-reverse seal assembly is under the cup plug assembly. You'll need a modified No. 4 Easyout to remove it from the case. Grind ¾ inch from the end of the Easyout before using.

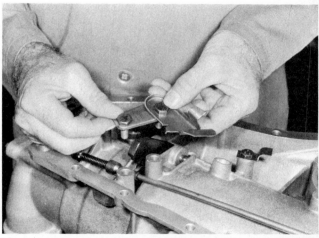

12. Unbolt and remove the dipstick stop/parking lock bracket. The entire transaxle is metric, so you'll need metric sockets and wrenches to work on it properly.

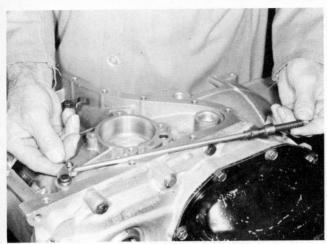

13. Pull the actuator rod end from the case, and swivel it as shown to align the tanged end with the slot cutout in the attaching arm. Depress the rod end and remove it from the attaching arm and case.

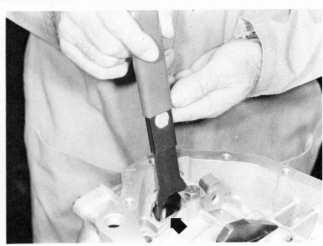

14. Rotate the final drive unit until the C-ring can be seen in the access slot (arrow). Align the C-ring so its open side faces the window. This special tool frees the ring from the output shaft.

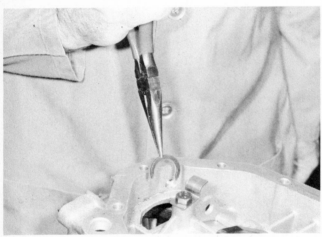

15. Turn the output shaft approximately 180 degrees and reach into the access window with needle-nose pliers. Grasp the C-ring, pull it off the shaft, and discard. Install a new C-ring upon reassembly.

16. Once the C-ring is removed, the output shaft can be withdrawn from the case without difficulty. Removing the C-ring is difficult without using the special tool.

17. Examine the output shaft for burrs, scoring, or other damage. Note that the ends are different. When the shaft is replaced in the case, the short splined end goes in first.

18. Rotate the transaxle so the case cover is up and remove the control valve body cover and gasket from the case. Discard the gasket and clean the cover in fresh solvent.

19. Two screws hold the throttle lever and bracket assembly to the control valve body. Remove the lever/bracket assembly with the TV cable link (arrow) attached.

20. Except for the bolt shown, the pump cover bolts also hold the valve body to the case. Remove all valve body bolts, but leave this pump cover bolt untouched.

21. Lift the valve body straight up and off the transaxle case. Place it (machined side up) on a workbench and note the difference in bolt lengths as you remove them.

22. To check the pump gears, remove the remaining cover bolt and lift cover off. The pump is a vane-type unit and disassembly/reassembly of components can be very tricky.

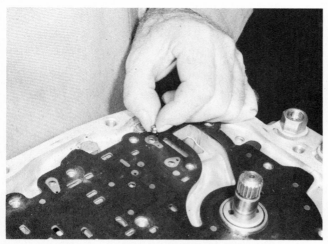

23. Locate the No. 1 check ball on the spacer plate and remove it from the case. The spacer plate is gasketed on each side. Keep this check ball separate from others in the case.

24. Lift the spacer plate/gasket assembly from the transaxle case. Discard the old gaskets and clean the spacer plate in fresh solvent before reassembly.

25. Withdraw the oil pump shaft from the transaxle case. The oil pump is quite reliable and should give no trouble, but inspect the shaft carefully just the same.

26. The transaxle case contains five check balls located in the circled areas. Note the location of each and remove the balls—do not mix up with the No. 1 check ball.

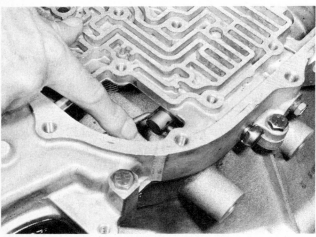

27. Disconnect the manual valve rod from the manual valve by depressing the rod. The spring clip on the rod will pop off the valve, separating the two with no difficulty.

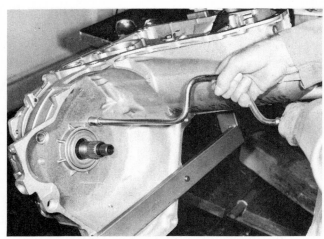

28. Remove the two case cover screws and washers from the converter housing side. Then remove the remaining case cover screws. Dip the screws in ATF before reinstalling to prevent galling the aluminum threads.

29. Lift the case cover from case. Invert and place the cover on the workbench. The 1-2 accumulator will face up. The 1-2 accumulator pin may fall out. Remove/discard the gasket.

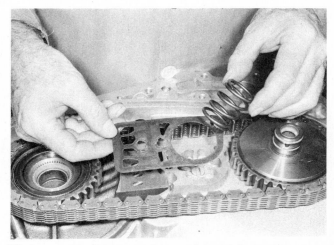

30. Remove the 1-2 accumulator spring and the center case-to-case cover gasket. Discard the gasket and inspect the Teflon oil seal rings on the drive sprocket shaft.

31. The drive sprocket thrust washer may remain attached to the case cover. If not on the drive sprocket shaft, check inside the cover for the nylon washer shown here.

32. When reassembling the case cover to the case, attach the nylon drive sprocket thrust washer to the cover as shown for easier installation—the washer presses into place.

33. If the 1-2 accumulator pin does not fall out of the case cover when the cover is removed, replace its oil seal rings, and then reinstall it in the cover bore.

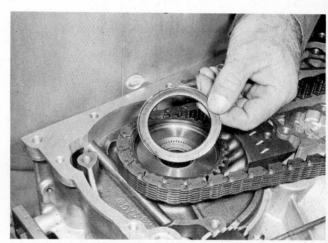

34. Remove the driven sprocket thrust bearing. When reassembling the transaxle, install the thrust bearing as shown on the drive gear. Thrust washer/bearing placement is very important.

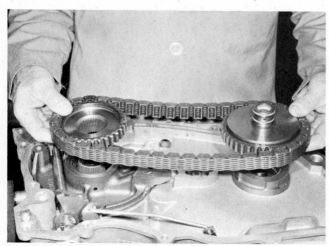

35. Jiggle the drive/driven sprocket assembly and lift up and out of the case with the link assembly as shown. Reinstallation is the reverse of removal.

36. The drive/driven sprocket-to-support thrust washers may remain in the case or come off with sprocket removal. In either instance, remove both thrust washers and inspect.

37. Rotate the detent lever toward the outside of the case and use a 3mm or ⅛-inch pin punch to remove the shaft roll pin. The pin will not come out with the detent lever in any other position.

38. Use a pair of needle-nose pliers to remove the manual shaft-to-case nail. If the nail is lost, it can be replaced with an ordinary nail of the proper length.

39. Withdraw the manual shaft from the transaxle case, then remove the detent lever/parking lock/manual valve rod assembly. When reassembling, insert the shaft through the case and into the assembly.

40. Remove the driven sprocket support and support-to-direct clutch housing thrust washer. The thrust washer may come out with the support. Replace the Teflon oil seal rings on the support shaft.

41. Remove the band anchor plug from the case and use needle-nose pliers to lift the intermediate band from case. Check the band surface and set it to one side.

42. Hold the input shaft and remove the direct and forward clutch assemblies. This unit is quite heavy, so use both hands.

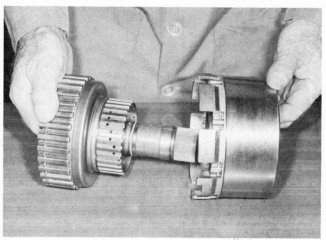

43. Separate the direct and forward clutch assemblies by simply pulling them apart. You can work on the clutch assemblies as you remove them, or all at one time.

44. We'll show you clutch disassembly and inspection now. All clutches are serviced in essentially the same manner. Pry the direct clutch snap ring from the clutch housing.

45. Turn the clutch housing upside down and tap gently to remove the backing plate and clutch pack. Separate the steel and composition plates for inspection.

46. Another snap ring must be removed to gain access to the clutch housing piston. When reinstalling the snap rings, make sure they snap into the proper groove all the way around.

47. Remove the apply ring and release spring assembly. Check the springs for distortion and/or damage. This is serviced as a single unit if replacement is required.

48. Turn the clutch housing upside down again and tap gently to free the direct clutch piston. Replace inner/outer piston seals and install a new housing center seal.

49. To reassemble the clutch, replace the piston, apply/release spring assembly, and snap ring. Alternate steel and composition clutch plates, install backing plate (flat side up), and snap ring.

50. To continue transaxle disassembly, remove the input internal gear-to-shaft thrust washer. This may be located on the end of the input shaft. The notched side faces up.

51. Withdraw the input internal gear from the case. Each component should be inspected and placed on the workbench in the order removed from the case for ease in reassembly.

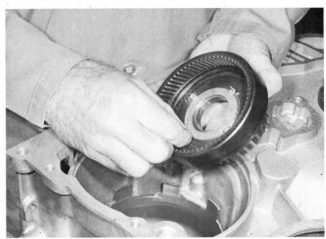

52. The input carrier-to-input internal gear thrust washer may be located on the underside of the internal gear instead of remaining with the carrier assembly.

53. Remove the input carrier assembly from the case. Check to see that the carrier-to-sun gear thrust washer is in position when reassembling the transaxle.

54. The input sun gear is the final component to be removed from the input drum. The sun gear can be replaced in the input drum with either side facing upward.

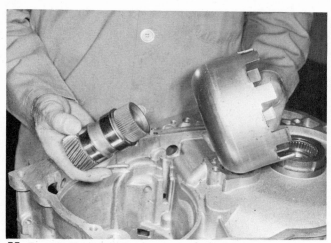

55. Remove the input drum and reaction sun gear from the transaxle case. Don't think the case is empty—there's still plenty to be removed, but you need special tools at this point.

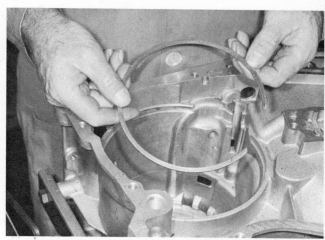

56. Remove the low/reverse clutch housing-to-case snap ring. Before further disassembly is possible, you'll need the help of a special tool.

57. GM tool J-28542 and adapter are required to separate the clutch assembly from the reaction carrier. Don't try removal without this tool or you're in real trouble.

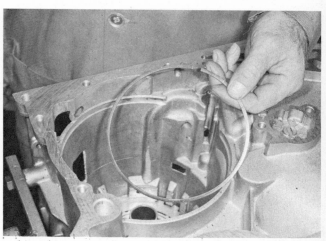

58. With the low/reverse clutch housing removed from the case, pry the housing-to-case spacer ring free and remove. All snap and spacer rings should be inspected.

59. Grasp the final drive sun gear shaft and pull the reaction gear set out of the case. We'll also show you how to service this type of holding member.

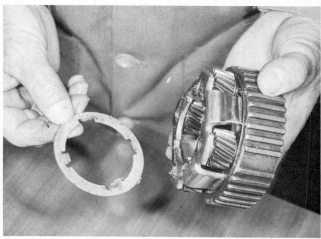

60. Remove the roller clutch/reaction carrier from the case and separate the tanged carrier-to-internal gear thrust washer from the end of the reaction carrier.

61. You'll find another thrust washer on the roller clutch side of this assembly. Inspect the roller clutch for wear, damage, or faulty operation.

62. Remove the low/reverse clutch plates from the final drive sun gear shaft. Inspect the composition plates for wear/damage. Dip new plates in ATF before installation.

63. Remove the reaction internal gear-to-reaction sun gear and thrust bearing assembly from the reaction gear. All thrust bearings should be separated and inspected for wear.

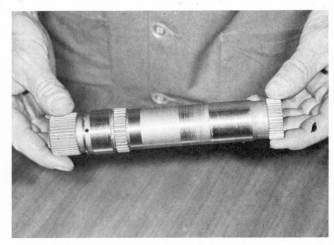

64. Remove the reaction internal gear from the final drive sun gear shaft. Inspect the shaft carefully for wear or damage and replace oil seal rings with a new set.

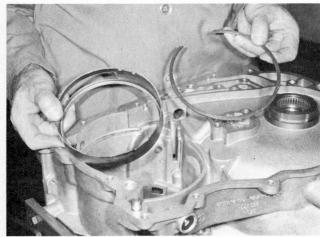

65. Pry the final drive internal gear spacer-to-case snap ring loose and remove it from the case with the final drive internal gear spacer as shown above.

66. When reinstalling the final drive internal gear spacer/snap ring, position the spacer so that the parking pawl will enter the slot in the spacer freely, as shown here.

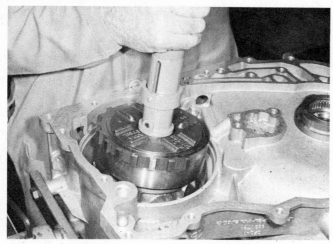

67. Another special GM tool (J-28545) is required to remove the final drive assembly from the transaxle case. Don't try to remove it without this tool.

68. Remove the final drive differential-to-case thrust selective washer and differential carrier-to-case thrust bearing from the final drive—these may remain in the case.

69. Separate the final drive internal gear from the differential case by rotating as you lift up. The differential is serviced as a complete unit (except for pinions) if anything is wrong with it.

70. You'll find another thrust bearing located inside the final drive unit. As with other thrust bearings, separate and check the bearing for wear/damage.

71. Remove the final drive sun gear and sun gear-to-differential carrier thrust bearing. The thrust bearing outside diameter race should face against the carrier when reinstalled.

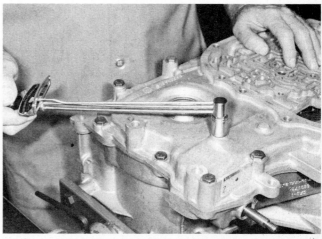

72. Reverse the procedure above to reassemble the transaxle, taking note of special reassembly instructions already covered. Torque the case cover bolts to 18 ft.-lbs.

1. To change the fluid/strainer, remove the front and side oil pan bolts. Loosen the rear bolts and pry the front of the pan down to drain the fluid into a suitable container.

2. As the fluid drains from the pan, continue loosening the rear bolts to let the pan tip forward and drain the rest of the ATF. Lower the pan carefully and dump whatever fluid remains.

3. Let the strainer continue draining before removing it. Note how the strainer is held in position against the dipstick stop. The new strainer must be positioned in the same way.

4. Rotate the strainer to the rear and pull down hard. There should be an O-ring seal on the attachment nipple; if not, reach into the bore (arrow) and remove it.

5. Install the new O-ring which comes with the factory replacement strainer. Slip the O-ring over the nipple of the new strainer and make sure it seats properly around the groove.

6. Position the new strainer and press the nipple into the bore (A) until fully seated. Swivel the strainer until it's properly located against the dipstick stop (B).

7. Use a putty knife or spreader to clean the old gasket residue from the oil pan flange. Wash the pan with clean solvent and blow dry with compressed air or wipe dry with a paper towel.

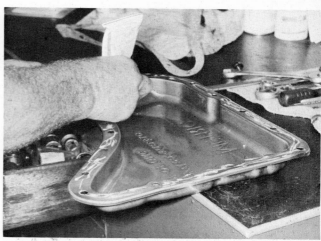

8. Factory replacement strainers come with a new pan gasket. To assure a proper fit, run a thin bead of gasket sealer around the pan mating flange.

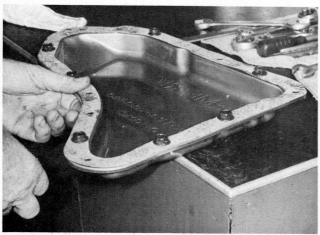

9. Position the new gasket on the pan and install pan bolts as shown to align the gasket holes with the pan. Press the gasket down until the sealer holds it in place.

10. Remove the pan bolts and reinsert two bolts as shown. These will be used as locating pins to position the pan/gasket properly on the transaxle case flange.

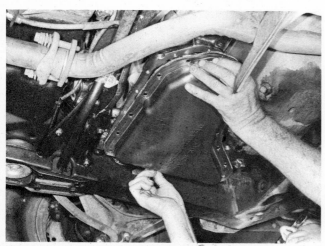

11. Hold the pan under the transaxle case and thread the locating pan bolts in place finger tight. Check to see that the other bolt holes line up and then tighten both bolts.

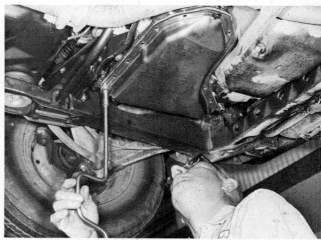

12. Install the remaining pan bolts and torque to 12 ft.-lbs. Lower the car and add 4 quarts of Dexron II ATF. Start the engine and let it idle in Park—DO NOT move the selector through the gear ranges. Let the engine idle for five minutes before shifting the gears.

12

Suspension and Steering

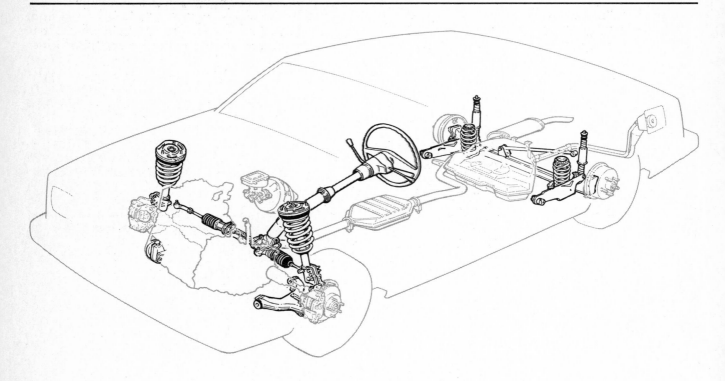

X-car suspension differs considerably from that used with rear-wheel drive cars. The X-car front suspension is a modified MacPherson design using a combination strut and shock absorber. The upper end of the strut is attached to a strut mount which extends into the engine compartment while the lower end connects to the steering knuckle.

A trailing-arm design is used for the rear axle assembly. The two control, or trailing, arms welded to the axle housing mount it to the body. Two coil springs support the car's weight, while double-action shock absorbers control road shock. The track bar is used to control sideward movement of the rear axle assembly. When equipped with the Super-lift leveling feature, these air-operated units are mounted in the same location as the conventional rear shock absorbers.

While all X-cars use this basic suspension design,

there is some difference in suspension tuning between the marques. This, however, does not affect suspension service, as long as you do not attempt to do something like replace Pontiac parts with the "same" components from a Buick dealer. As long as you do not have the misfortune to jump a curb, or otherwise apply a great deal of shock to the strut assemblies, they will deliver good service with only periodic shock absorber replacement. Damaged struts cannot be straightened but must be replaced.

The quickest way to determine if the shocks are up to par is the time-honored car shake. With all four wheels on the ground, apply a vigorous up-and-down motion to one fender at a time and watch the car's reaction when you suddenly stop. If the fender vibrates once or twice, then comes to rest, the shock is working satisfactorily. If the fender continues to vibrate without your assistance, you need new shocks.

To adjust camber, loosen the cam (arrow) and through-bolts. Rotate the cam bolt to move the upper knuckle and wheel in or out to specs; then torque to 140 ft.-lbs.

Replacing the front shock absorbers is a job beyond the do-it-yourselfer. Strut disassembly requires the use of special equipment and should not be attempted without the special compressor tool, as it is extremely dangerous. Rear shocks are another story. They can be replaced with no more difficulty than any other shock absorber. You simply open the deck lid, remove the trim cover, and unbolt the top end of the shock. Jack the car up, support the rear axle assembly on a jackstand, and remove the lower bolt and nut.

Wheel Alignment

To keep your X-car in safe operating condition, the wheels must be properly aligned. Wheel alignment is another job you should not try to do at home, since it also requires special equipment. But you should understand the factors which affect alignment and how to spot danger signs. In this way, you can determine when a quick trip to the wheel alignment shop is necessary. This will prevent excessive wear that eventually leads to expensive suspension repairs at best, and to a potentially dangerous operating condition at worst. Since the latter is an open invitation for an accident, it pays to be informed.

There are five angles or factors involved in front wheel alignment: caster, camber, toe-in or toe-out on turns, and steering axis inclination. Unlike other cars you may have owned, the modified MacPherson strut suspension of your X-car permits adjustment only of camber and toe. The other angles are design functions of the suspension, but they should be checked on the alignment rack to determine if there are any worn or bent parts which need replacement. Toe-in and toe-out refer to the relationship of the wheels to each other when the steering is in a straight-ahead position. A slight amount of toe is required to compensate for the effect of camber, which tends to force the two wheels away from each other at the forward edge when rolling.

What to Look For

If your car doesn't seem to handle as it should, there are several checks you can make before settling on the suspension as being at fault. First, check your tires for correct inflation. As simple as this sounds, the amount of air in your tires has much to do with how the car performs. At the same time, take a close look at your tire wear pattern. Wear located primarily on one side indicates toe-in or camber problems. If incorrect toe-in affects just one wheel, the car will tend to pull to one side or the other. Incorrect toe-in of both wheels will make it difficult to steer in either direction. Worn shocks, a bent spindle, a misaligned wheel, or a combination of these will cause tire cupping.

The wheel bearing assemblies at each wheel are factory-lubricated, adjusted, and sealed during manufacture. When excessively worn, the entire hub and bearing assembly must be replaced—they cannot be adjusted. To check the play in the front wheel bearings, jack the car up to keep the ball joints under tension. Then grab the upper and lower surfaces of the tire and shake it—vigorously at first, and then gently. The vigorous shaking will determine if there is unacceptable wear in the suspension; the gentle movement will show bearing play. A slight movement is acceptable, but anything over .005 inch indicates the need for a new bearing.

The only accurate way to determine if the play is within acceptable limits is to remove the tire and wheel. When checking the front bearings, remove

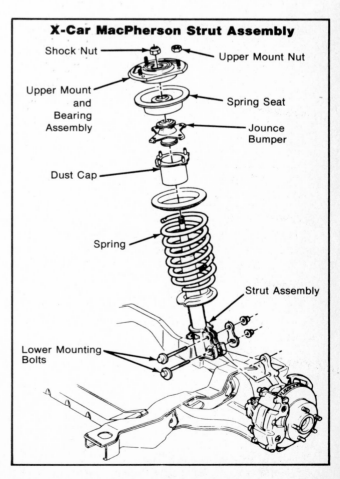

X-Car MacPherson Strut Assembly

Shock Nut — Upper Mount Nut

Upper Mount and Bearing Assembly — Spring Seat

Jounce Bumper

Dust Cap

Spring

Strut Assembly

Lower Mounting Bolts

Suspension and Steering

the brake caliper and replace two nuts to hold the disc to the bearing. Mount a dial indicator as shown on page 141. If you're working on the rear bearings, the brake drum will have to come off to mount the dial indicator as on page 141. In either case, the amount of push-pull movement will produce a reading on the dial indicator. If the reading is greater than .005 inch, the entire hub and bearing assembly should be replaced.

Steering gear problems can also contribute to poor handling. X-cars use a rack-and-pinion steering arrangement which can be adjusted if necessary. To adjust the steering box, loosen the adjuster plug lock nut and tighten the plug until you feel it bottom out lightly. Back the plug out about 45 degrees from the bottomed position and retighten the lock nut. This should restore the steering to normal, unless the gearbox components are excessively worn. Turn the steering wheel from lock to lock. If it binds at any point, loosen the adjuster plug enough to free the binding action; then torque the lock nut to 50 ft.-lbs.

To make this adjustment on the X-car steering gear, you really need access to a hoist, as well as lots of patience. The steering gearbox is mounted up against the bottom of the firewall (see page 141), and access to the adjuster plug is rather limited. If you find it easier to remove the steering box and tie rod assembly for this adjustment, secure the gearbox in a soft-jaw vise and remove the adjuster plug and spring. Lift the rack bearing from the housing and check it for wear. Replace the bearing, spring, and plug, tightening it until you feel it bottom. Back off the plug 45 degrees and use an in.-lbs. torque wrench to turn the pinion. Turn the adjuster plug in

The power steering pump on the L4 engine is hidden below the air conditioning compressor. We removed the radiator to show you its relative position. Adjustments are made from under the car.

or out as required until the torque wrench shows a preload of 8 to 10 in.-lbs. to turn the pinion; then replace the adjuster plug lock nut and torque it to 50 ft.-lbs.

The popular power steering option is similar in appearance and design to the manual box, but it contains a number of extra parts, including several lip seals that are prone to failure on occasion. These seals are found on the steering rack and pinion at the rack, at the pinion and hydraulic valve,

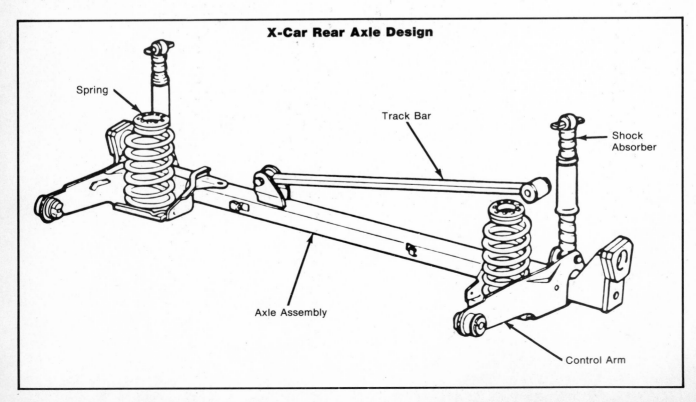

X-Car Rear Axle Design

Spring

Track Bar

Shock Absorber

Axle Assembly

Control Arm

and on the pump driveshaft. Whenever leakage occurs in one of these areas, the seals must be replaced, after the sealing surfaces have been cleaned and inspected. If severe pitting of the shaft is found, it must be replaced. Slight corrosion can be corrected by cleaning the shaft surface with crocus cloth.

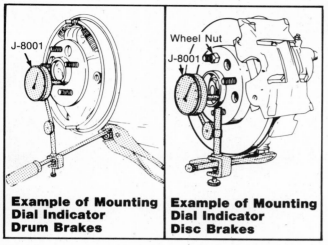

Example of Mounting Dial Indicator Drum Brakes

Example of Mounting Dial Indicator Disc Brakes

Any sudden demand for power steering fluid, combined with a loss of power assist but no leak spots under the car, indicates a seal failure. The fluid is being pumped to the steering box, where it leaks past the seal(s) and settles in the tie rod boot seals. If you suspect a seal leak, pull the left front wheel and check the boot seal. When filled with fluid, it becomes greatly distended and puckers at the retaining clamp end. Since this is not an uncommon occurrence, we've prepared a pictorial sequence at the end of this chapter to help you replace the seals.

The major problem in overhauling either gearbox is getting it out of the car. Below shows you how it's mounted. One caution, however—remove the bracket nuts carefully. If you happen to pull one of the mounting studs out in the process, you've got a real problem. The studs remain in the bottom of the firewall and serve as locaters for replacing the supports, steering box assembly, and brackets properly and easily. Lots of patience is necessary during removal and replacement, but the job is not beyond the capability of anyone who wishes to take the time and save the money.

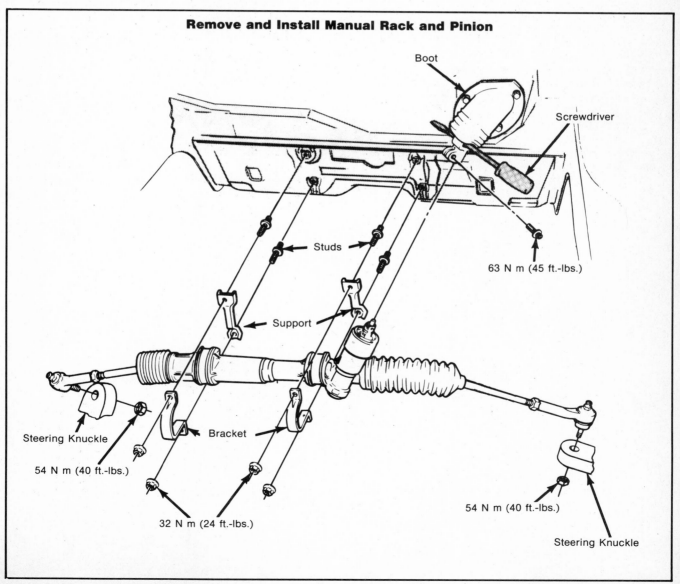

Remove and Install Manual Rack and Pinion

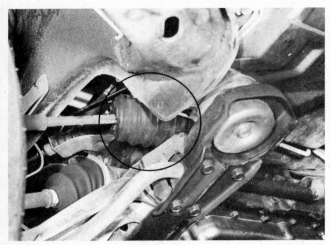

1. When the power steering unit develops a seal leak, the boot fills with fluid and swells out of shape.

2. The first step is to puncture the boot with an ice pick and let it drain, then squeeze out any remaining fluid.

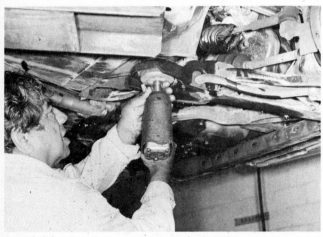

3. Remove the rear cradle bolts, support the cradle with a transmission jack, and disconnect the tie rod ends from the steering knuckle.

4. All hoses and lines as well as the steering column-to-intermediate shaft bolt are removed from topside—it's slow work.

5. The lowered cradle gives better access to the support brackets. Remove the brackets from underneath and withdraw the assembly.

6. Remove the rubber grommets and breather line, support the rack in a soft-jawed vise, and slide the nylon ring off the tie rod housing.

7. The tie rod housing is staked in two places. Use a hacksaw to cut through the staked area on each side of the housing.

8. Finish removing the staking with a small punch and hammer. This should allow the tie rod housing to turn freely with a wrench.

9. Fit the wrench over the flat on the tie rod housing and turn counterclockwise until the tie rod separates from the rack.

10. Repeat steps 7-9 on the other tie rod; then remove the adjuster plug lock nut and unscrew the adjuster plug from the housing.

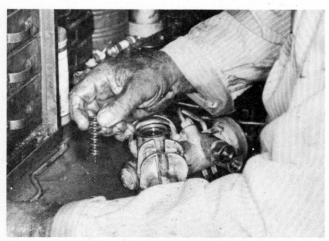

11. Remove the spring and rack bearing. You may have to rotate the rack back and forth to free the bearing for removal.

12. Clean and inspect the rack bearing. If corroded or excessively worn, the bearing should be replaced.

13. Pry the dust seal from the bottom of the pinion shaft housing and remove the lock nut. Equalize the rack length at each end with the stub shaft.

14. Mark the stub shaft flat location on the housing and press—do not hammer—the threaded end of the pinion free from the housing.

15. Work the pinion and valve assembly free from the housing carefully. This is no time to be in a hurry.

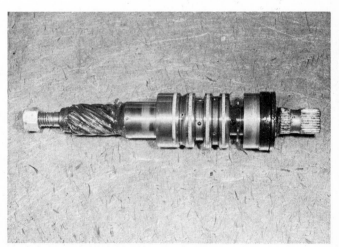

16. Inspect the pinion/valve assembly for signs of wear/damage. Replace the valve body rings if necessary.

17. Removing the bulkhead retaining ring is also a slow and tedious job. Install a punch in the access hole and pry the ring free.

18. Separate the rack and housing. The inner rack seal will remain inside the housing while the piston ring stays on the rack.

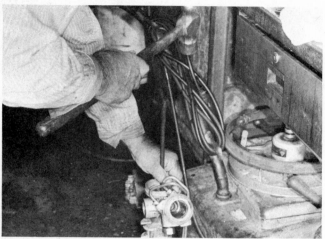

19. Using a rod about 12 inches long, tap gently with a hammer to remove the inner rack seal from the housing.

20. Here's a look at the rack seal/nylon insert. Lip seals such as this seal rotating shafts and require special treatment.

21. Inspect the rack carefully. If it shows any signs of pitting, corrosion, wear, or damage, it must be replaced.

22. When corrosion in the lip seal contact area is slight, clean the shaft with crocus cloth.

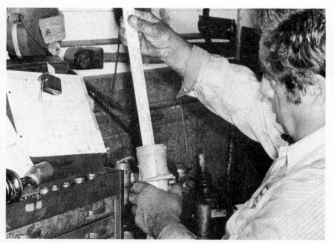

23. Measure to the flange inside the housing, install the seal/insert after lubricating with power steering fluid, and remeasure to make sure the seal/insert is properly seated.

24. Once the rack seal is properly seated in the housing, replace the O-ring seal in the outer bulkhead.

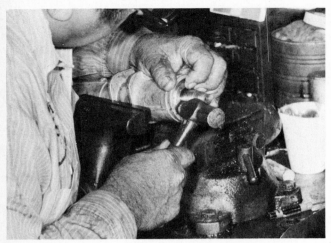

25. Install the rack in the housing and replace the outer bulkhead. Tap lightly with a hammer to assure proper seating.

26. Fit the retaining ring in position on the bulkhead end and install it in the housing groove. Make sure it's properly seated.

27. Equalize the rack and install the valve/pinion assembly so the stub shaft flat and housing mark align when the assembly is seated.

28. Install the seal, dust ring, and retaining ring. Several light taps on an appropriate-size socket should seat the ring.

29. Turn the housing over in the vise and install the dust cover and lock nut. Seat the lock nut and torque to 26 ft.-lbs.

30. Install the rack bearing, spring, and adjuster plug. Bottom the plug lightly, back it off 40-60 degrees, and install the lock nut.

31. Attach the tie rod housing to the rack, tighten the housing snugly, and restake in two places. Fit the nylon ring over the housing.

32. Replace the other tie rod in the same manner, staking the housing in two places.

33. If the nylon ring does not fit easily over the tie rod housing, tap it in place with a hammer.

34. Install the breather tube, fit the inner boot over the housing and tube, and then slide a new clamp in place.

35. Squeeze the clamp with pliers to draw it tightly around the boot. Install rubber grommets on the housing.

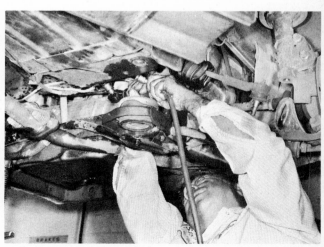

36. Replace the housing in the car and install the support brackets. Attach the tie rods, fluid lines, and steering column. Bleed and refill the system.

13

The Engine

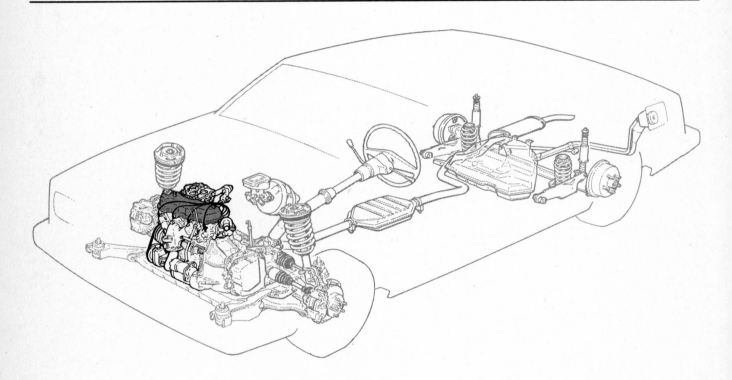

ooner or later, every automotive engine reaches a point where an overhaul of some kind is necessary. With some, it's simply a case of old age and hard work finally catching up. Others quit when they blow a head gasket or throw a rod. In either case, the solution is an overhaul or rebuild.

For most of us, engine work is out of the question. It requires a considerable number of specialized tools and equipment not generally found in the average home garage. While you can rent the necessary tools and equipment, high rental costs and the time involved in engine rebuilding make it more economical to let your dealer do the work. For this reason, we've limited photo coverage in this chapter to a typical head removal/replacement sequence. This would be necessary to replace a blown head gasket or do a valve job.

Since these jobs require considerable labor and only about $30 worth of parts (not including the

valve grind), you can save money on a valve job by removing/replacing the head yourself, while paying a professional to grind the valves and valve seats to specifications. The GM flat rate manual specifies 3.7 to 4.7 hours of labor for removing one head from the V6 engine, depending upon how the car is equipped. Using this as a general guideline, multiply the figure by the shop's hourly rate to find out how much you can save by pulling the head yourself.

As for special tools, about all you'll need are an air compressor/air wrench and a valve spring compressor. The air wrench is not really a necessity, but it will speed up the job and save a lot of wear and tear on your arms. It also has the advantage of reaching into tight places to pull a bolt that could otherwise be difficult to remove with ordinary hand tools. The valve spring compressor is necessary only if you want to strip the head down yourself. If you don't, simply turn it over to an engine rebuilder and let him do the stripdown/reassembly along with grinding the valves.

You'll need a head gasket for each head removed, as well as an intake manifold gasket for the V6. (The L4 manifolds and V6 exhaust manifolds do not require gaskets.) These gaskets are all sold separately, as General Motors does not offer a valve grind gasket set for either engine. In addition, a tube of RTV sealant (GM P/N 1052366) is required. This sealant is used with the two-piece V6 intake manifold gasket, as well as with all rocker arm/valve covers. Parts departments are notorious for their inefficiency, so be prepared to insist that GM *does* manufacture a 2.8L V6 engine.

The following pictorial sequence shows the major steps involved in removing and replacing the right, or rear, cylinder head on a 1980 V6 Citation engine. Many of the same steps are involved in removing the L4 head. In addition, we've provided the proper valve action and torque specs for both engines. All that's required now is a little elbow grease—and you provide that!

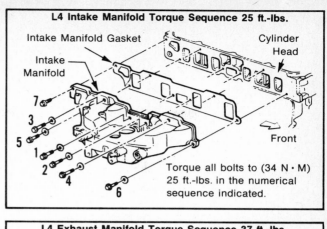

L4 Intake Manifold Torque Sequence 25 ft.-lbs.

Intake Manifold Gasket

Intake Manifold

Cylinder Head

Front

Torque all bolts to (34 N·M) 25 ft.-lbs. in the numerical sequence indicated.

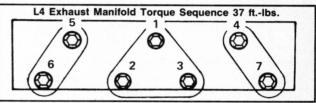

L4 Exhaust Manifold Torque Sequence 37 ft.-lbs.

Valve grinding requires special equipment and is no job for an amateur.

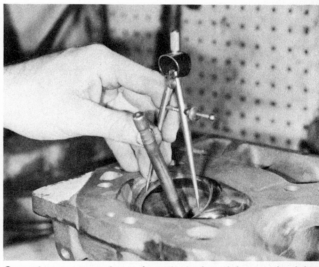

Correct measurements are important when doing a valve job.

Refacing and dressing valve seats must be done properly.

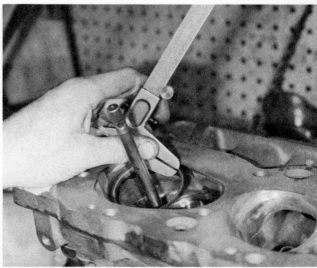

Seat angle and runout must be kept within specified tolerances.

Valve Specifications

Valve Action / Timing

Intake Valve Timing

Disp.	Rocker Ratio	Lobe Lift (Int. / Exh.)	Opens (°BTC)	Closes (°ABC)	Duration (Degrees)
2.5L	1.75	.406/.406	33	81	294
2.8L	1.50	.587/.667	25	81	286

Intake Valves & Springs

Disp.	Intake Overall Length	Intake Head Diameter	Intake Stem Diameter	Intake Stem To Guide Clearance
2.5L	4.924	1.72	.3418-.3425	.0010-.0027
2.8L	4.70	1.60	.3409-.3417	.0010-.0027

Exhaust Valves & Springs

Disp.	Exhaust Overall Length	Exhaust Head Diameter	Exhaust Stem Diameter	Exhaust Stem To Guide Clearance
2.5L	4.489	1.50	.3418-.3425	.0010-.0027
2.8L	4.738	1.30	.3409-.3417	.0010-.0027

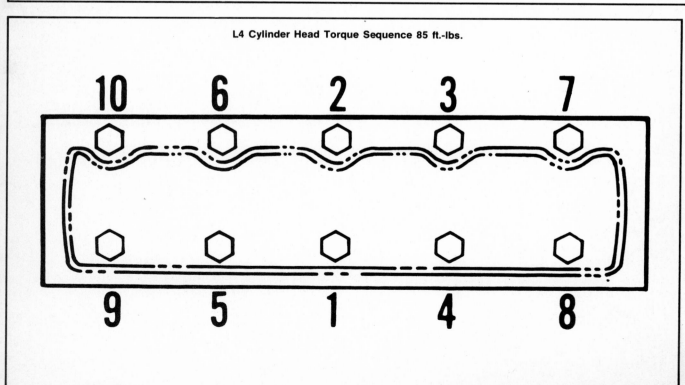

L4 Cylinder Head Torque Sequence 85 ft.-lbs.

Exhaust Valve Timing

Opens (°BBC)	Closes (°ATC)	Duration (Degrees)	Overlap (Degrees)	Valve Lift Zero Last (Int./Exh.)
76	38	294	71	.404/.404
69	55	304	80	.347/.393

Intake Outer Springs Pressure & Length		Intake Inner Springs Pressure & Length		Angle Of Seat/Face (Des.)
Closed (lb. @ In.)	Open (lb @ In.)	Closed (lb. @ In.)	Open (lb. @ In.)	
78-86 @ 1.66	122-180 @ 1.254	—	—	46/45
88 @ 1.61	195 @ 1.16	Damper	Damper	46/45

Exhaust Outer Springs Pressure & Length		Exhaust Inner Springs Pressure & Length		Angle Of Seat/Face (Des.)
Closed (lb. @ In.)	Open (lb. @ In.)	Closed (lb. @ In.)	Open (l.b. @ In.)	
78-86 @ 1.66	122-180 @ 1.254	—	—	46/45
88 @ 1.61	195 @ 1.16	Damper	Damper	46/45

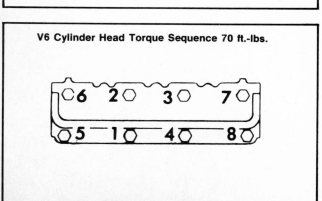

V6 Intake Manifold Torque Sequence 23 ft.-lbs.

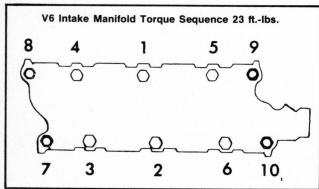

V6 Cylinder Head Torque Sequence 70 ft.-lbs.

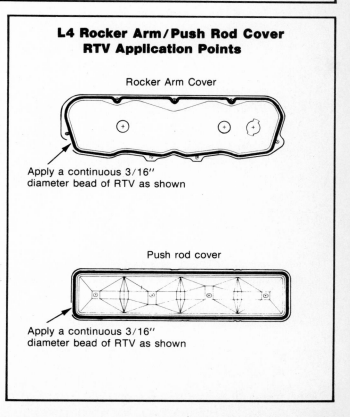

L4 Rocker Arm/Push Rod Cover RTV Application Points

Rocker Arm Cover

Apply a continuous 3/16″ diameter bead of RTV as shown

Push rod cover

Apply a continuous 3/16″ diameter bead of RTV as shown

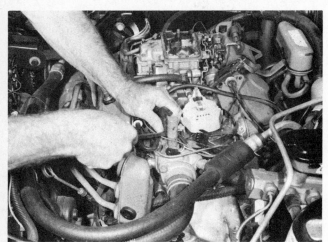

1. While the engine coolant is draining, remove the air cleaner housing and distributor cap with plug wires attached. Disconnect vacuum lines and electrical leads.

2. When engine support strut is removed, the V6 will lean slightly toward radiator, but not enough to make strut reinstallation difficult.

3. Remove the left, or front, rocker cover attaching screws. To reach the screw on the end of the cover facing the air conditioning compressor, remove the bracket (arrow).

4. When all screws have been removed, loosen the rocker cover by tapping it with a rubber mallet. Do not try to pry the cover free with a screwdriver.

5. Here, sealant is used instead of a gasket. Lift the rocker cover up and angle as necessary for removal. Remove the rear rocker cover as in the previous steps.

6. The Pulsair valve attaching bracket must be disconnected from the rear rocker cover to swing it out of the way. Loosen, but do not remove, the bracket screw under the valve housing.

7. Unbolt the distributor hold-down, align the rotor with the carburetor, and lift up. The rotor will move, so mark the new rotor position with chalk to assist installation.

8. Disconnect the manifold from the manifold pipe from underneath vehicle; then remove the two nuts holding the EFE valve line to the intake manifold. Disconnect and plug the fuel line.

9. Remove the intake manifold attaching bolts.

10. Insert a pry bar as shown, and lift the intake manifold up to break gasket seal. Since the manifold is aluminum, pry carefully to avoid any chance of damage.

11. Once the gasket seal is broken, grasp the intake manifold at each end and lift up and off engine. The manifold is very light and can be easily handled by one person.

12. Loosen the rocker arms and remove the pushrods in pairs. Place them aside in the sequence removed so they can be replaced in the same order as removed.

13. If both heads are to be removed, repeat the previous step. Remove cylinder head bolts. If you find any green fluid (antifreeze), soak it up with a cloth before removing head.

14. Insert the pry bar at one end of the head as shown and pry gently to break the gasket seal. The head is now ready to be removed from the block.

15. Grasp the head as shown and lift up. The exhaust manifold and Pulsair system will come off the engine with the cylinder head. This is heavier than intake manifold, so hang on tightly.

16. Place the head on a clean surface and unbolt the exhaust manifold. This engine design does not use an exhaust manifold gasket, but the L4 does.

17. To remove the valves from the head, remove rocker arms, install valve spring compressor, and remove each pair of valve locks. Place parts in a small container for safekeeping.

18. Release the compressor and remove the spring retainers, spring shield, springs, dampers, and oil seal. Repeat process on remaining valves.

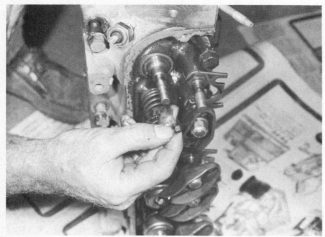
19. Inspect the oil seals carefully. This engine only had 6000 miles on it, but the oil seals had already dried out and cracked. New seals should be installed.

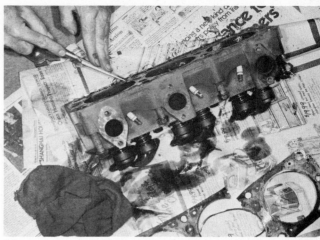
20. Pull off the old gasket and clean the head surface of all remaining gasket material. Clean the intake manifold and rocker cover flanges of gasket and sealant residue.

21. Carefully clean residue from the block mating surfaces. You should have compressed air available to blow residue out of the piston cylinders and off the block.

22. Remove the dowel pins from the cylinder head and install them in the block. These position the new gasket properly and hold it in place during head installation.

23. Replace the valves if removed. Reattach the exhaust manifold to head and carefully lower head on block, taking care not to scuff or move the new gasket out of position.

24. Tighten the cylinder head bolts gradually, following the sequence shown. The final head bolt torque should be 70 ft.-lbs. The proper torque and tightening sequences are essential.

25. Now install the new intake manifold gaskets. If the pushrods are not removed, the top edge of the gasket must be cut as shown for a proper fit. Install the pushrods and tighten the rocker arms.

26. Front and rear of block do not use a gasket. Run a thin (5mm) bead of sealant along each mating flange and extend it ½ inch onto the end of the gasket.

27. Carefully lower the intake manifold into position. Install the attaching bolts and torque them to 23 ft.-lbs., following the tightening sequence shown.

28. Tighten the rocker arm nuts to eliminate lash. With the engine in the No. 1 firing position, adjust E1, 2, 3 and I1, 5, 6 valves. Adjust others with engine in the No. 4 firing position.

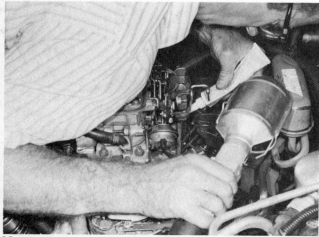

29. Run a thin (3mm) bead of sealant along the head sealing surface. Run the sealant on the inboard side of the bolt holes. Sealant in the holes can cause a "hydraulic" condition and head damage.

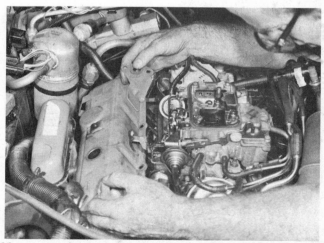

30. Install the rocker covers while the sealant is wet, and torque the bolts to 8 ft.-lbs. The remainder of the process is simply one of replacing/reconnecting. Finally, time the engine (see tune-up section).